GUIDE TO THE JOHN D. CRUMMEY

PEACE COLLECTION

IN THE HOOVER INSTITUTION

GUIDE TO THE JOHN D. CRUMMEY PEACE COLLECTION IN THE HOOVER INSTITUTION

Compiled by

George Esenwein

HOOVER INSTITUTION
STANFORD UNIVERSITY
1991

The Hoover Institution on War, Revolution and Peace, founded at Stanford University in 1919 by President Herbert Hoover, is an interdisciplinary research center for advanced study on domestic and international affairs in the twentieth century. The views expressed in its publications are entirely those of the authors and do not necessarily reflect the views of the staff, officers, or Board of Overseers of the Hoover Institution.

Hoover Press Bibliography 75

Copyright 1991 by the Board of Trustees of the Leland Stanford Junior University

All rights reserved. No part of this publication may be reproduced, stored in a retrieval system, or transmitted in any form or by any means, electronic, mechanical, photocopying, recording, or otherwise, without written permission of the publisher.

First printing 1991

Manufactured in the United States of America.

Library of Congress Cataloging-in-Publication Data

John D. Crummey Peace Collection (Hoover Institution on War, Revolution, and Peace)
Guide to the John D. Crummey Peace Collection in the Hoover Institution / compiled by George Esenwein.
  p. cm. -- (Hoover Press bibliography ; 75)
Includes bibliographical references (p.   ) and index.
ISBN 0-8179-2752-2
1. Peace--History--Sources--Bibliography--Catalogs. 2. John D. Crummey Peace Collection (Hoover Institution on War, Revolution, and Peace)--Catalogs. I. Esenwein, George Richard. II. Title. III. Series
Z6464.Z9J57   1991
[JX1952]
086.3271'72--dc20   91-16234
                                     CIP

The illustration on the title page, "Swords into Plowshares," is from a publication of the Civilian Public Service Camp during World War II.

The image of the dove on the cover is a detail from a European youth movement's poster commemorating an "international day of youth and student solidarity."

CONTENTS

Acknowledgments vii

Introduction 1

User's Glossary 14

Part I. Special Collections 15

Part II. Organizations 76

Part III. Serials 89

Bibliography 116

Index 118

Hand-painted anti-war posters from the Hoover Institution's collection of the National Circulating Library of Original Peace Posters.

"Peace Means Progress" (U.S. Collection)

"Together for the World's Peace" (1939; Yukio Tashiro, artist)

ACKNOWLEDGMENTS

The preparation of this guide was made possible by a grant from the United States Institute of Peace, Washington, D.C. While assembling it, the compiler has drawn heavily upon the previously published surveys of the Hoover Institution's area collections that are listed in the bibliography. Charles Palm, associate director of the Hoover Institution, and William Ratliff, curator of the International and Americas Collections, generously offered their advice and expertise. Other staff members of the Stanford University Libraries, SUL and the Hoover Institution who provided valuable suggestions are: Elena Danielson, associate archivist; Peter Duignan, Sara and Ira Lick Curator; Joseph Dwyer, deputy curator of Russian and Eastern European Collections; Peter Frank, curator, Germanic Collections, (SUL Green); Edward Jajko, assistant curator, Middle East Collection; Jim Knox, assistant chief, General Reference, (SUL Green); Neil McElroy, head, Readers' Services; Molly Molloy, Slavic librarian, Readers' Services; Agnes Peterson, curator of Central and West European Collections; Dale Reed, deputy archivist; and Maciej Siekierski, deputy curator, Eastern Europe Collection. Much of the project involved a great deal of technical work that I could not have easily accomplished without the assistance of others. I should therefore like to thank Marja Lutsep and especially Kent Eaton for the countless hours they spent cheerfully and conscientiously helping me with editing, researching and word-processing tasks. The manuscript also greatly benefited from the technical advice and editorial assistance I received from Dana Harris of the Hoover Institution Computer Systems Office, and Janet Shaw, Marshall Blanchard and Pat Baker of the Hoover Institution Press.

George Esenwein
International and Americas Collection

"Peace on a Pedestal" (1919; V. Prouve, artist; from the French Poster Collection)

INTRODUCTION

BACKGROUND OF THE PEACE COLLECTIONS

Events of the twentieth century have been largely shaped and conditioned by world wars, civil wars, and other varieties of armed conflict. Yet this same period has also witnessed the rise and fall of countless individual and collective initiatives aimed at bringing an end to all wars. While most of these antiwar movements were shortlived, the ideas and values that both inspired and sustained them have survived in one form or another, not least because of the existence of institutions (mainly in Europe and North America) that have sought to collect and preserve peace-related documents.[1] Thanks to the foresight of some, like the founders of the Hoover Institution at Stanford, California, a considerable part of the historical record of twentieth-century peace efforts will not be lost to future generations.

The idea of creating permanent repositories for peace materials, however, was slow to develop in many countries. In the United States this was primarily because peace societies of all types have tended to be preoccupied, not with gathering and preserving documents, but rather with promoting peace

---

[1] I am referring here, not to the numerous peace research centers that have emerged in the post Second World War period, but rather to the handful of institutes and libraries that have been systematically collecting on peace from the turn of the century onward.

through public demonstrations, legislative reforms, educational programs, and the like. Even organizations that have made a special effort to maintain their own archives -- notably the Fellowship of Reconciliation, the War Resisters' League, the Women's International League for Peace and Freedom, and the World Without War Council -- have eventually found it expedient to deposit their records with public academic institutions. Today nearly all the major archival collections relating to peace activism and peace organizations are located at research libraries scattered across the country, such as those at Columbia University, Duke University, the New York Public Library, Swarthmore College, and the Wisconsin Historical Society, among others. [2]

One of the earliest and largest repositories of peace materials in North America was the Hoover Institution at Stanford University, which was founded in 1919 through the initiative and financial support of Herbert Hoover, the thirty-first president of the United States.[3] Mr. Hoover apparently first conceived of the idea of creating a library in 1914 after having read some remarks by Andrew D. White, president of Cornell University, on the difficulties he had faced in finding fugitive literature and other primary sources on the French Revolution. Deeply impressed with the fact that the loss of contemporary historical evidence might possibly prevent future historians and social scientists, as well as the general public, from learning more about the nature and significance of such pivotal events, Hoover resolved to do

---

[2] See, Marguerite Green, compiler and editor, Peace Archives: A Guide to Library Collections. (World Without War Council, 1986).

[3] The Hoover Institution was originally a special department within the Stanford University library system, but it quickly developed into a library in its own right. In 1922 it became the Hoover War Library, but the name was later changed several times, becoming in turn, the Hoover Library on War, Revolution and Peace (1937-1942); the Hoover Library on War, Revolution and Peace and Hoover Research Institute (1942-1946); Hoover Institute and Library (1946-1957); and currently, Hoover Institution on War, Revolution and Peace.

what he could to conserve the documentary record of World War I. Nearly five years later his plan finally materialized in the form of the Hoover War Collection.

In the beginning, the Library's main activity was defined as the acquisition of documents relating to the study of the "causes, conditions, and consequences of war." Implicit in this policy, especially as far as Mr. Hoover himself was concerned, was the view that the study of war was an interdisciplinary enterprise which should not be restricted to only one area of investigation. Partly for this reason, the administrators at the budding Institution soon decided to enlarge the scope of the Library's research activities and collecting interests so that it embraced all forms of social, political, and economic change in the twentieth century – including the study of peace. By defining its scholarly mission so broadly, the Hoover Institution rapidly distinguished itself from other libraries of comparable standing, such as France's Musée de la Guerre, Britain's Imperial War Museum, and other national war libraries, whose main occupation has been to document and commemorate the war experiences of individual countries.

There is a further reason peace collections have always formed an integral part of the Hoover Library. Having served as the head of the Commission for Relief in Belgium (CRB) and then as the director general of relief for Allied and associated powers following the armistice in 1918, Mr. Hoover was made keenly aware of the appalling toll that war took on the lives of people and on society generally. A Quaker with pacifist convictions, Hoover strongly believed that, if it were ever possible to avoid the tragedy of human conflict, it would be necessary to collect and preserve all the materials available on the subject. In practice, this meant accumulating not only materials strictly about war, but also a vast array of documents that could be used both to record and to foster the development of global peace. Speaking at the dedication of the Hoover Tower on 20 June 1941, Mr. Hoover affirmed that the Library's resources on peace lay at the heart of the collections:

> Here can be found the record of the ideas and forces which made for failure of the last peace and the ideas and forces which might have made its success. Out of these files the world can get great warning of what not to do and what to do when it next assembles around the peace table . ... Surely from these records there can be help to mankind in its confusions and perplexities, and its yearnings for peace.
> The purpose of this institution is to promote peace. Its records stand as a challenge to those who promote war. They should attract those who search for peace.[4]

This speech, which was delivered on the eve of America's involvement in this century's most devastating war, set forth a goal of the Hoover Institution that future administrators would strive to implement.[5] In keeping with the aims of its founder, a central concern of the Institution continues to be the problem of securing and maintaining peace.

Currently the Hoover Institution Peace Collection -- now known as the John D. Crummey Collection on Peace -- comprises over 8,000 books, 300 serials and newspapers, 838 posters, and more than two million pages of archival materials relating to peace.[6] The fact that the Library and Archives also possess unparalleled collections on twentieth-century wars and revolutionary movements (events which have until now been the principal determinants of

---

[4] Dedication of The Hoover Library on War, Revolution, and Peace. (Stanford, 1941), pp. 38-39.

[5] See, for example, Glenn Campbell's foreword to The Library of the Hoover Institution, (Stanford, 1985), pp. vii-viii.

[6] In 1977 this collection was formally established by the FMC Corporation with a grant to the Hoover Institution, and was named after the corporation's founder, John D. Crummey.

peace), means that the Hoover Institution can justifiably claim to be among the largest and most comprehensive research centers on peace in the world.

PEACE COLLECTIONS AT THE HOOVER INSTITUTION

The Hoover Library's first significant acquisition on peace, which formed the nucleus around which later collections were built, was the set of materials known as the "Authentic Delegation Propaganda at the Paris Peace Conference, 1919." The collection, numbering some 2,000 titles, was gathered between May and October, 1919 by the Stanford historian Dr. Ephraim Adams and other representatives of the Hoover War Collection, as it was then called. It consists mostly of pamphlets, leaflets, and other documents presented to the Paris Peace Conference by 53 delegations. In addition, there are many items that were distributed by this group of delegates as propaganda. These publications addressed a variety of issues that had been thrown into sharper relief by World War I, not least being boundary disputes, indemnifications for aggressions, and national self-determination. Although this collection is not complete -- owing in part to the fact that some delegations had left Paris before the Stanford/Hoover team began its work -- it contains many publications that are exceedingly rare or unique.[7] Some of the document groups represented in this section are: the minutes of the plenary sessions of the Supreme Council (including the Council of Ten, the Council of Five, and the Council of Heads of Delegations); and one of only 40 privately printed sets of David Hunter Miller's My Diary at the Conference of Paris, with Documents, a 21-volume record of the various councils and committees of the conference. The Institution eventually received the complete records of the Paris Peace Conference -- totalling 87 linear feet of publications -- as well as

---

[7] Introduction to a Bibliography of the Paris Peace Conference, pp 3-4.

microfilm of related materials that only became available during the 1970s.

During the first three decades of this century, when antiwar movements arose and spread across the globe, the Institution acquired several major collections on peace. One of these was the extensive archive and library of David Starr Jordan, a prominent American peace activist and first president of Stanford University (1891-1913). Because he was a close friend and colleague of Herbert Hoover, Dr. Jordan also played a role in the early development of the Hoover Library. In 1919 he donated his "Plan of Education for Peace" to the Library, and similar gifts were made until his death in 1931. All his correspondence with American and foreign members of the international peace movement, the unpublished manuscripts of his speeches and notes and other documents were willed to the Institution. In addition to these unpublished materials, his collection includes over 500 books and pamphlets on peace and internationalism.

Other substantial collections focusing on early twentieth-century peace movements in Europe and America -- especially from the point of view of women participants -- are those of Ada Morse Grose, a member of the Henry Ford Peace Expedition (1915) and the Neutral Conference for Continuous Mediation (Stockholm, 1916); Alice Park, another American delegate to the Ford Peace Ship Expedition; and Rosika Schwimmer, a Hungarian pacifist and feminist who was awarded the World Peace Prize in 1937.

Before the outbreak of World War II the Library obtained the papers and personal library of Alfred Hermann Fried (1864-1921), an Austrian jurist and dedicated pacifist who received the Nobel Peace Prize in 1911. Fried's collection, which comprises over 2,500 items, offers a comprehensive history of peace movements from 1892 to 1921. Among other things, it includes the manuscript of Fried's war diary (18 volumes) and parts of the library of Bertha von Suttner, a leading figure in the European peace movement during the closing years of the nineteenth century. A former secretary to Alfred Nobel, Suttner achieved international recognition as the author of the antiwar novel, Die Waffen Nieder! (Lay Down Your Arms!), which, more than any other single work of the period, helped to mobilize public opinion against war.

Efforts to secure a lasting peace during the interwar years (1919-1939) are thoroughly documented. For example, the Library owns a wide-ranging collection of publications issued by the dozens of international and national peace societies that flourished at this time — the Association to Abolish War and the Buffalo Peace and Arbitration Society, for example. Since many of these were only tiny groups that frequently disappeared as quickly as they had arisen, the documentary record for these organizations is often fragmentary, consisting mainly of extremely scarce circulars, leaflets, and similar kinds of ephemera.

The Library also houses records that trace the origins and development of the League of Nations, which came into existence in 1920 and held its final meeting in 1946. Because the Hoover Institution was designated as a depository library for the League, it holds nearly complete runs (supplemented by microfilm) of such publications as the Official Journal (1920-1940), Annuaire de la Société des nations (1920-1938), Société des nations revue mensuelle documentaire (1920-1926), and the League's Treaty Series (1920-1946), which was subsequently taken over by the United Nations. The collection also includes comprehensive documentation of the League's subsidiary organizations, the World Court — beginning with the Procès-verbal (1920) of the League Advisory Committee of Jurists on the Permanent Court of International Justice — and the International Labour Organisation (ILO).

Documents relating to multinational disarmament initiatives undertaken during the inter-war period represent yet another dimension of the peace collections. Two rare items of this type that deserve mention are the proceedings of the Conference on the Limitations on Armaments (Washington, D.C., 1921-1922), and the verbatim report of the second plenary session of the Conference of Naval Armament (Geneva, 1927).

The records of the activities of pacifists and conscientious objectors in America during the Second World War (1939-1945) can be found in several archival collections, including those of the American Friends Service Committee, Church of Brethren, and The Fellowship of Reconciliation.

Since World War II the size and scope of the peace collections have continued to expand. Subjects range from the early history of the United Nations, to domestic and international antiwar movements, to contemporary world disarmament efforts. The New Left Collection is an outstanding example of the type of special document groups acquired in the post-war period. This remarkable set of materials, which began in 1968 as a joint effort between the Hoover Institution and the Stanford University Libraries, contains the policy statements, position papers, underground and alternative newspapers, posters, and other primary sources that reflect the New Left movement's position on such topics as the draft (draft resistance and conscientious objection), the war in Vietnam, and pacifism.

Throughout the post World War II era the focus of the Curators' collecting activities has shifted in response to the ever-changing pattern of world conflict. While making a concerted effort to document peace activism in Europe from 1945 on -- especially among communist-sponsored youth groups based in Eastern Europe -- the curators have paid special attention to the peace movements that have sprung up outside of North America and Europe. For example, soon after the Japanese formally surrendered in 1945, representatives of the Stanford University Alumni Association of Tokyo began accumulating documents that shed light on the social and political forces that had plunged the nation into war. Records of the activities of nonviolent and pacifist groups that subsequently emerged in Japan were also gathered together, and these can be found in the Institution's Western and East Asian collections.

Another example of this trend has been the gathering of primary and secondary sources pertaining to various Central American peace movements that were launched during the 1980s. Documentation associated with several major peace initiatives which were aimed at ending civil strife in the region, including the Oscar Arias Peace Plan, are housed in the Library and Archives.

Although the threat of another world war may have receded in recent years, this has not rendered the study of peace irrelevant. On the contrary, regional conflicts -- particularly in Third World countries -- show no signs of abating, and the possibility that such disturbances might develop into larger wars and even spread to other parts of the globe is an inescapable reality. The search for peace will no doubt remain a constant feature of the world's political landscape, and, for this reason, the Hoover Institution plans to continue the development of its peace collections.

ORGANIZATION OF THE GUIDE

Despite their richness and diversity, the Institution's peace collections have been difficult to use. Access has been limited in part because much of the material on peace is submerged in larger collections that relate primarily to other subjects. Until now, only partial inventories of the Institution's peace resources have been available to scholars. Published more than 50 years ago, these are bibliographical guides to the Paris Peace Conference of 1919: A Catalogue of Paris Peace Conference Delegation Propaganda in the Hoover War Library (1926), and An Introduction to a Bibliography of the Paris Peace Conference (1935).

This, then, is the first general survey of the Institution's peace holdings. It is intended primarily as a research tool for finding peace-related materials that are dispersed throughout the Institution's multinational collections. The user should note that this is a descriptive guide of certain collections rather than a bibliographical listing of the vast number of books, pamphlets, and other publications housed in the Library and Archives.

As defined by the Library of Congress classification system, the subject "peace" encompasses a broad range of topics. For the purposes of this guide, the related subjects of international law, diplomacy between individual nations, military science and history, and all that is commonly associated with the post-World War II concept of "peace through strength" have been excluded. Relief programs, such as those with which Herbert Hoover was affiliated during and following World War I, also fall outside the scope of this guide. The principal subject areas represented here are those pertaining to international cooperation and the arbitration of disputes, peace settlements and movements, disarmament and arms control, pacifism and pacifist organizations, and twentieth-century antiwar activism. It deserves mention that some individuals and organizations who have themselves never pursued peace as a fundamental goal are listed below because their records have had (or have) an important bearing upon peace movements. Among the divergent groups found in this category are the Communist Information Bureau and the National Security League.

Following this overview of the history and development of the Hoover Institution's peace collections, there are three bibliographical sections.

The first and largest one describes materials that have been designated as "Special Collections." These are our principal collections related to peace housed in the Archives and the Library. For the most part these consist of official documents, files of organizations, the personal papers of persons active in the public life of the United States and other countries, and miscellaneous documents gathered by individual collectors. As will be seen, they vary in size, nature and origin. When consulting Part I, the user should keep in mind the following information:

(a) A special collection may contain an assortment of items in various formats, including books (manuscript or printed), personal documents (typescripts, hand-written letters, etc.), official records, serial publications (newspapers and journals in hardcopy or microform), and special materials such as pamphlets, broadsides, leaflets, memorabilia (artworks, campaign buttons, currency, etc.), posters, photographs, documentary films, and phonograph records.

(b) The collections grouped together in this section can be found in the Institution's Library and Archives, which are administered separately. As a rule, "Special Collections" are housed in only one of these two locations. However, if an individual collection is divided, summaries of its holdings in both the Library and Archives have been provided.

(c) Several microfilm collections on peace owned by Stanford University Libraries have been included because they contain documents that are integrally related to special collections at the Hoover Institution. Two examples are the Jane Addams and Emily Greene Balch microfilm collections, which contain many items that complement the Institution's important holdings on David Starr Jordan and the Women's International League for Peace and Freedom. For information on the sizeable collection of materials (books, periodicals, and microfilm) on peace housed in the Stanford University Libraries, the user should consult with the Reference Division of Green Library.

(d) In a few cases we have indicated only the general nature of the collection, but in all others the following data for each entry is provided: the collection's size, span of dates, format, topics covered, language (other than English), location, and the restrictions, if any, for research use.

Part II is a list of the national and international organizations and societies on which the Library holds ephemeral files of primary and secondary materials. As a rule, these document groups are smaller and less comprehensive than those found in Part I. The organizations in this section range from peace associations -- such as, the Chicago Peace Society and World Peace Council -- to religious and secular bodies that have been involved in peace efforts. The latter category includes groups as disparate as the Friends World Conference Committee, the Communist International and the United Nations, organizations whose conceptions of peace, if not totally dissimilar, usually have had little in common with one another.

Serial publications that are housed in the Hoover Library, including current subscriptions and titles no longer received, are listed in Part III. While most of the peace-related serials at the Institution are represented here, the list is by no means exhaustive. Not included are titles belonging to exceptionally large collections -- like that of the League of Nations -- nor those that have been cited in the section on "Special Collections."

The Institution's extensive holdings on peace are further strengthened by over 830 peace posters, dating from the turn of the century and continuing up to the present. These are located in the Archives, where they can be found among the various national and international poster collections. Information about each poster's size, distinguishing features, and place of origin can be obtained from the Institution's in-house computer database. The posters themselves have been cataloged and are available for study or purchase on slide transparencies.

The primary purpose of this guide is to publicize the diverse collections on peace that are available for consultation at the Hoover Institution. To this end, we hope that it will prove useful to other libraries; to potential donors looking for the appropriate depository for their collections; and, above all, to scholars and others interested in pursuing research on peace.

The Dove: Universal Symbol of Peace

An European youth movement's commitment to peace is represented in this poster commemorating an "international day of youth and student solidarity."

Pablo Picasso's rendering of a peace dove for the World Congress for General Disarmament and Peace (Moscow, 1962)

A post-World War II French poster attempts to ridicule communist politics by depicting a dove in the shape of a tank.

USER'S GLOSSARY

*Main entries are arranged alphabetically. These include (1) personal names, (2) corporate names, and (3) topical names of collections.

*All Cyrillic names have been transliterated.

*Note on cross-reference symbols -- Superscripts:

"i" = see also, special documents.
"ii" = see also, organizations.
"iii" = see also, serials.
"i, iii" = see also, special documents and serials.
"ii, iii" = see also, organizations and serials.

PART I: SPECIAL COLLECTIONS

ABRAMS, IRWIN, 1914- Papers, 1902-1989.
13 ms. boxes.

American educator; director, foreign service training, American Friends Service Committee, 1943-1946; director, Quaker Overseas Work Camps, 1946-1947; vice president and president, International Society for Educational, Cultural and Scientific Interchanges, 1976-1982.
Archive summary:Speeches and writings, correspondence, reports, minutes, bulletins, newsletters, curricular material, and other printed matter, relating to activities of the American Friends Service Committee, International volunteer work camps, conscientious objection during World War II, education in Germany, International educational and cultural exchanges, especially between the United States and East and West Germany, and the Nobel Peace Prize.
Indexes: Register.

ADAIR, FRED LYMAN, 1877-1972 Papers, 1918-1942. 8 ms. boxes, 3 envelopes, 2 phonorecords.

American physician; Red Cross relief worker in Belgium, 1918-1919.
Archive summary: Correspondence, reports, photographs, notes, and printed matter, relating primarily to activities of the American Red Cross in Belgium, 1918-1919, and to the America First Committee, 1940-1942.
Indexes: Register.

ADDAMS, JANE, 1860-1935 The Jane Addams Papers, 1860-1960 [microform] / [Mary Lynn McCree Bryan, editor; editorial group, Peter Clark, et al.]. Ann Arbor, Mich.: University Microfilms International, 1984. 82 microfilm reels; 35 mm.

Social reformer, feminist, and Nobel laureate in peace in 1931, Addams was chairperson of the American Women's Peace Party and the Women's International League for Peace and Freedom (The Hague).

Stanford University Libraries,[8] Microtext MFILM N.S. 3911 (Library has v.1-71 (Reels 1-71);v.72-82 (Addendum reels 1-11)) Bryan, Mary Lynn McCree. University of Illinois at Chicago. University Microfilms International.
NOTES: "The University of Illinois at Chicago ... served as 'host' institution for the project." — Acknowledgements. For contents consult user's guide: The Jane Addams Papers (HV28.A35A24), located in Current Periodicals/Microtext. See also, BALCH, EMILY GREEN; GRUBBS, FRANK LESLIE; JORDAN, DAVID STARR.

AHLBORN, EMIL. Holograph Letter, 1917, to CHARLES F. DOLE. 1 folder.

Archive summary: Relates to the origins of World War I, and to American entry into the war.

ALLEN, THEOPHILUS. Holograph Letter, 1926, to CHARLES D. MARX. 1 folder.

Archive summary: Relates to the prospects for German admission to the League of Nations.

ALLIED AND ASSOCIATED POWERS (1914-1920) TREATIES, 1918-1920. 1 ms. box.

Archive summary: Conclusion of World War I. Countries represented: United Kingdom of Great Britain and Ireland, Austria, Austria-Hungary, Bulgaria, Germany, Hungary, Romania, and Turkey.
Indexes: Preliminary inventory.

ALMOND, NINA, Collector. Collection, 1919-1920. 1 ms. box. typed transcript.

Archive summary: Bulletins, reports, and memoranda, published in "The Treaty of St. Germain: A Documentary History of Its Territorial and Political Clauses, with a Survey of the Documents of the Supreme Council of the Paris Peace Conference," edited by Nina Almond and Ralph Haswell Lutz

---

[8]The microforms described here and below are held in the Green Library of the Stanford University Library system.

(Stanford: Stanford University Press, 1935).

AMERICA FIRST COMMITTEE.[ii] Records, 1940-1942.
338 ms. boxes, 7 oversize boxes, 20 photographs, 50 posters, 2 motion picture film reels, 1 video cassette, 2 film strips, 26 phonorecords.

Private organization lobbying for U.S. nonintervention in World War II.
Archive summary: Correspondence, minutes of meetings, reports, research studies, financial records, press releases, speeches, newsletters, campaign literature, form letters, clippings, mailing lists, films, photographs, and phonorecords.
Indexes: Register.

AMERICA FIRST COMMITTEE. FIGHT FOR FREEDOM COMMITTEE. Records, 1940-1942.
5 ms. boxes.

Archive summary: Correspondence, memoranda, press releases, pamphlets, clippings, and printed matter, relating to the interventionist and non-interventionist movements in the U.S. during World War II, the America First Committee, and the activities of Charles Lindbergh and Herbert Hoover in the non-interventionist movement.

AMERICAN CIVIL LIBERTIES UNION (Including Northern and Southern California Branches).

New York group founded in 1920 by the social activist Roger Baldwin and others. The stated purpose of the ACLU is to champion the "rights of man set forth in the Declaration of Independence and the Constitution."
Library summary: 34 books, 1 report, 1 bibliography, papers, 97 society publications, 17 pamphlets, 1 address, 1 leaflet, 10 serials.

AMERICAN FRIENDS SERVICE COMMITTEE.[ii,iii] (AFSC) See also, CIVILIAN PUBLIC SERVICE (a.k.a., FRIENDS CIVILIAN PUBLIC SERVICE). Records, 1941-1945. 4 ms. boxes.

Quaker organization established in 1917 to coordinate the

various bodies of the "Friends" in the United States. Dedicated to the search for world peace through disarmament and nonviolent social change, the AFSC was a co-recipient of the Nobel Peace Prize in 1947.

Archive summary: Civilian Public Service Records, including memoranda, newsletters, and reports concerned with the issue of conscientious objection in the United States before and during World War II.

Library summary: 69 books, including reports, laws, testimony, summary of proceedings, reprints of articles; 1 4-volume report; 1 newsletter; 2 bulletins, 1941-1944; background material, program in China, irreg. 1946, Dec. 1948-1950; periodic summary, program in China Oct. 1948-Mar. 1950; program in Finland Mar. 27, 1959; program in India Mar. 1948; program in India and Pakistan 1948-1949; program in Japan Aug. 1948, June 1949; Annual Report irreg. 1921-1965; 41 pamphlets; 93 society publications; German Relief News; Progress Reports; International Affairs Report; Numbered Bulletins, 1-299; 4 unnumbered bulletins; Personnel directory, 1944-1945; 3 newsletters; Civilian Public Service (microfilm); News from Germany and Austria irreg. 1947-1955; AFSC reporter irreg. 1961-1971; 2 articles; 1 report; unlisted material.

AMERICAN FRIENDS SERVICE COMMITTEE.[iii] PACIFIC SOUTHWEST REGION. See, BETTY COLE, Coordinator of the Peace Studies Program, Pacific Southwest Region, AFSC.

AMERICAN LEAGUE AGAINST WAR AND FASCISM.[ii,iii] [a.k.a., AMERICAN LEAGUE FOR PEACE AND DEMOCRACY].

Established in 1933 by a coalition of liberals and left-wing organizations, the ALAWF was largely dominated by members of the CPUSA, (Communist Party, United States). In 1937 the ALAWF changed its name to the American League for Peace and Democracy.

Library summary: 5 books; Bulletin, irreg. 1945-1948; 22 society publications; 7 pamphlets; 1 biographical file; Chart of Resolutions; thesis on microfilm; 1 reel of microfilm; 1 3-volume report; American Legion; 18 books; Chart of Resolutions; thesis on microfilm; 1 reel of microfilm; 1 3-volume report; Georgia: 2 books; Iowa: 1 book; National American Commission: 2 books; National Executive Committee: 1 book; New York: 1 book; Rhode Island: 1 book; Special Committee (Human Rights): 1 book; Virginia: 1 book; 9 society publications; 1 society publication in French; 8

pamphlets; 22nd, 23rd, 25th convention proceedings; 1 poster; 1 radio script; 3 speeches; 1 memo; 1 bulletin; 6 envelopes, unlisted material, including pamphlets.

AMERICAN PEACE SOCIETY,[ii,iii] **1884-1917.**

Established in 1828, the APS was an association of several regional peace groups that sought to promote international peace. It was active throughout most of the nineteenth century and continued its work until 1980.
Library summary: 7 books; 6 pamphlets; essay; 9 leaflets, including poems; 1 reprinted article; 1 paper.

AMERICAN SONGS OF PEACE. 1 phonorecord.

American songs relating to peace, 1767-1940, performed by John Swingle.

AMERICAN UNION AGAINST MILITARISM[ii,iii] **(Also variously known as Anti-Prepardness Committee, Truth About Preparedness Committee, and The League for an American Peace.)**

Founded in New York in 1915 as the Anti-Militarism Committee. The AUAM opposed militarism and conscription during the 1915-1922 period.
Library summary: Fact flyer; New York State laws; 2 speeches of Daniel Webster; 32 society publications, incl. articles; 3 envelopes unlisted material; leaflets 1-7; society publication, Great Britain; 8 pamphlets; article of suggestions for 1916-1917; 1 debate; addresses; unlisted material.

AMERICA'S TOWN MEETING OF THE AIR (Radio program) broadcast, 1945. 2 phonorecords.

Archive summary: Relates to the founding of the United Nations and its prospective role in ensuring world peace.

BAKER, ELIZABETH N. Miscellaneous papers, 1938-1966. 1 folder.

Archive summary: Leaflets, bulletins, correspondence, and clippings, relating to U.S. politics and government, and conservative, anticommunist, and pacifist political groups in the United States. Indexes: Preliminary inventory.

BAKER, GEORGE BARR, 1870-1948. Papers, 1919-1932.
14 ms. boxes.

American journalist; a director of the American Relief Administration.
Archive summary: Correspondence, photographs, and printed matter, relating to the American Relief Administration; Commission for Relief in Belgium; Paris Peace Conference; U.S. presidential politics and the 1924, 1928, and 1932 presidential campaigns; Calvin Coolidge and Herbert Hoover; the Republican Party; and the foreign language press.
Indexes: Preliminary inventory.

BALCH, EMILY GREENE, 1875-1961. The Papers of Emily Greene Balch, 1875-1961 [microform] / editor, Martha P. Shane. Wilmington, DE: Scholarly Resources, 1988. 26 microfilm reels; 35 mm.

A founding member of the Women's Trade Union League of America, an associate of the Women's International League for Peace and Freedom (1919), and secretary general of the International Women's League in Geneva until 1922, Balch was awarded the Nobel peace prize in 1946.
Stanford University Libraries, Microtext MFILM N.S. 8035
NOTES: Organized into three sections: (1) biographical, (2) correspondence, (3) diaries, journal, notes, etc. "Published in cooperation with the Swarthmore College Peace Collection, Swarthmore, Pennsylvania." For contents consult user's guide: Papers of Emily Greene Balch 1875-1961, guide to the scholarly resources microfilm edition / editor Martha P. Shane, located in Current Periodicals/Microtext.
See also, ADDAMS, JANE; GRUBBS, FRANK LESLIE; JORDAN, DAVID STARR.

BEDFORD, HASTINGS WILLIAM SACKVILLE RUSSELL, 12TH DUKE OF, 1888-1953. Papers, 1942-1952. 1 ms. box.

British pacifist and author.
Archive summary: Pamphlets by the Duke of Bedford, 1942-1952, and correspondence between the Duke of Bedford

and Louis Obed Renne, 1948-1952, relating to pacifism and military disarmament.

BELL, JOHANNES. Typescript translation of a memorandum, n.d. 1 folder.

German diplomat.
Archive summary: Relates to the participation of the German delegation in the Paris Peace Conference in 1919. Translated by Alma Luckau.
English translation from German.

BLISS, TASKER H. Papers, 1918-1919. 1 folder.

General, U.S. Army; chief of staff, 1917; delegate, Paris Peace Conference, 1918-1919.
Archive summary: Correspondence and memoranda, relating to the American Commission to Negotiate Peace at the Paris Peace Conference; the military, economic, and political situation in Europe following World War I; and European relief and reconstruction. Includes correspondence with Herbert Hoover.
Indexes: Preliminary inventory.

BOTHA, LOUIS, 1862-1919. 1 ms. box. See, PEACE SUBJECT COLLECTION.

BOUSHALL, THOMAS C. "Stepping Stones of Peace from the Stumbling Blocks of War": Mimeographed Transcript of speech, 1944. 1 folder.

President, Morris Plan Bank of Virginia.
Archive summary: Relates to postwar reconstruction in the U.S. Delivered before the Rotary Club of Roanoke, Virginia, October 26, 1944.

BRIGGS, MITCHELL PIRIE. Collection, 1918-1930. 1 folder.

Archive summary: Manuscripts of writings, correspondence, and clippings, relating to the role of George D. Herron, an adviser to Woodrow Wilson, in formulating the World War I peace settlement, and to his subsequent views on European politics. Used by M. P. Briggs as research material for his book, George D. Herron and the European Settlement.

BROUGHTON, NICHOLAS, 1916- Papers, 1940-1947.
1 ms. box.

American conscientious objector during World War II. Broughton served at the Civilian Public Service Camp (No. 76) in Glendora, California between 1942-1946.
Archive summary: Memoirs of and records (newsletters and other printed matter) relating to conscientious objectors in the United States during WWII.

BUTLER, CHARLES A. "Senator, the Door is Closed":
Typescript history, 1950. 1 v.

Archive summary: Relates to American reaction to the Versailles Treaty and the Covenant of the League of Nations, 1919.

CAMPAIGN FOR NUCLEAR DISARMAMENT[ii,iii] **(Great Britain).**
Archives of the CND [microform]. Brighton, Sussex, England: Harvester Press, c1984-1986. 45 microfilm Harvester; 35 mm (Harvester/primary social sources. Left in Britain; pt.5 Campaign for Nuclear Disarmament).

British organization/movement launched in 1958 to protest the proliferation of nuclear weapons. Since its inception, the CND has sought to bring about world wide nuclear disarmament. NOTES: Publisher's note and contents at head of reel 1. Contents: Section 1: reels 1-16. 1958-1972 (excluding pamphlets and serials) -- Section 2: reels 17-25. 1973-1980 (including pamphlets and serials 1958-1980) -- Section 3: reels 26-45. 1981-1985 (including pamphlets and serials 1981-1985).

CARNEGIE ENDOWMENT FOR INTERNATIONAL[ii,iii] **PEACE**

Founded in 1910 by the industrialist/philanthropist Andrew Carnegie to look for ways to abolish war. The CEIP promotes

research and education in foreign policy issues, but especially those related to arms control and disarmament.
Library summary: Approximately 485 books, including reference lists, bibliographies, compilation of legislation, executive orders. International Law books, including 6 in "confidential print," official documents, treaties, and peace proposals. European Center: 14 books; Fiftieth Anniversary Publication (1957); Humanitarian Policy Studies: 2 books; Division of Intercourse and Education: 24 books, 31-volume bulletin, and set of 19 publications; Division of Economics and History: about 80 books, plus International Conciliation, 1930-38, irreg. Preliminary Economic Studies of the War, #'s 1-25; Belgian series #'s 1-7; French series #'s 1-51; and Austrian-Hungarian series #'s 1-19; Pamphlet series, 46 volumes; 2 reading lists; Issues before the General Assembly (1949-1970, 2nd - 25th General Assemblies); 18 pamphlets; 7 society publications.

CARNEGIE ENDOWMENT FOR INTERNATIONAL PEACE. CONFERENCE ON EXPERIENCE IN INTERNATIONAL ADMINISTRATION (1943: Washington, D.C.) Mimeographed proceedings, 1943.
1 v. (in 1 folder)

Conference held under the auspices of the Carnegie Endowment for International Peace.
Archive summary: Relates to postwar prospects for the League of Nations.

CARNEGIE ENDOWMENT FOR INTERNATIONAL PEACE. EXPLORATORY CONFERENCE ON THE EXPERIENCE OF THE LEAGUE OF NATIONS SECRETARIAT (1942: New York) Mimeographed proceedings, 1942. 1 folder.

Conference held under the auspices of the Carnegie Endowment for International Peace.
Archive summary: Relates to postwar prospects for the League of Nations.

CATT, CARRIE CHAPMAN.
Papers of Carrie Chapman Catt [microform] Washington, D.C: Library of Congress Photoduplication Service, [1983?] 18 microfilm reels; 4 in., 35 mm.

Leading spokesperson in the cause of world peace during the

interwar years.
Stanford University Libraries, Microtext MFILM N.S. 3594 (Library has Reels 1-18). Library of Congress.
NOTES: Unpublished papers held at the Library of Congress including items on women's suffrage, world peace, and women's rights, plus diaries, letters, and other materials collected by or pertaining to Mrs. Catt. Materials date from 1848 to 1950.

CHRISTOL, CARL QUIMBY, 1913- Herbert Hoover, the League of Nations and the World Court: **Typescript, 1974.** 1 folder.

Professor of International Law and Political Science, University of Southern California.
Archive summary: Paper presented at the Herbert Hoover Centennial Summer Seminar on the Presidency of Herbert Hoover, West Branch, Iowa, August 8, 1974.

CHURCH OF BRETHREN. BRETHREN SERVICE COMMISSION CIVILIAN PUBLIC SERVICE. Records, 1941-1946. 5 ms. boxes.

Pacifist religious organization affiliated with the Federal Council of Churches (1908-1950).
Archive summary: Memoranda, bulletins, newsletters, and reports relating to compulsory non-military public service, conscientious objectors, and the work of the Brethren Civilian Public Service Committee in the U.S. during WWII.

CIVILIAN PUBLIC SERVICE UNION (CPSU). Units, 1941-1946.

Union for drafted workers who were conscientious objectors. Organized in 1944 in the CPS camp at Big Flats, New York.
Library summary:

Unit 3: "The Patapsco Peacemaker," Oct. 1941-Dec. 1942
Unit 4: "The Olive Branch," May 1942-Dec. 1945
Unit 5: "Pike View Peace News," Sept. 1941-Jan. 1946
Unit 6: "The Salamonie Peace Pipe," Aug. 1941-Nov. 1943
Unit 7: "Magnolia Time Peace," Nov. 1941, Jan.-Feb. 1942
"Peace Pathways,"

March 1942, May 1942-Nov. 1942 publication on nutrition, May 1943
Unit 8: "Louise Whitaker Newsletter," April-May 1942
"Whispering Pines," March 1942, March 1943
Unit 9: "Days of Our Year," Sept. 1941-April 1942
Unit 10: "New Roots," Sept. 1941
Unit 13: "Peace Sentinel," 1942
Unit 14: "The Plowshare," June 1942, Jan.-Feb. 1943
Unit 15: "Salt," Jan. 1942, March 1942
Unit 16: "Kane Penn," Oct.-Nov. 1942
"Raising Kane," June/July 1944
Unit 19: "Calumet," Oct. 1941-May 1943
Unit 20: "The Turnpike Echo," March 1943
Unit 23: "Camp Coshocton," April 1942
"Seed," May 1942-March/April 1944
Unit 24: "The Soil," Feb. 1943
Unit 25: "Weeping Water News Drops," Aug., Dec. 1942, Jan. 1943
"On the Level," March 1943
Unit 27: Box 96, Feb.-March 1945 (Crestview, FL:)
"Crestviews," Aug. 1942-July 1943
"Wakulla Newsletter," April 1945 (Orlando, FL:)

"The Cultural Rag," March 1944-Feb. 1945
Unit 28: "Peace Sentinal," Sept. 1941-April 1946
Unit 30: "Camp Walhalla News," Jan. 1942-July/Aug. 1943
"School of Cooperative Living," Aug.-Oct. 1943
Unit 31: "The Snowliner," July 1942-April 1944 (irreg.)
Unit 32: "The Compass," Nov. 1942, Feb. 1943
"The Bulletin," Dec. 1942-Sept. 1943
"Action," March-June 1943
letter from Corbett Bishop
Unit 33: "Poudre Canon News," July 1942-Feb. 1943 (irreg.)
"Rising Tide," March 1943-Feb. 1945
Unit 34: "Harmony," Aug. 1942-Oct. 1943 (irreg.)
Unit 35: "High Sierra Vistas," Oct. 1942-Sept. 1944
Unit 36: "Manana," July 1942-March/April 1943
Unit 37: "Sage O'Pinon," Nov. 1942-Spring 1945
"The Mono Log," July 1942-Oct. 1942
Unit 42: "Builders," Sept. 1942-June 1944
"School of Cooperative Living," Nov. 1943-Jan. 1945
Unit 43: "Martin G. Brumbach Reconstruction Unit,"

Sept. 1942-April 1943
Unit 45: "Skyliner,"
Feb. 1943-March 1946
Unit 46: "Big Flats"
handbook
"Grass Roots," Sept. 1942-A.ug. 1943
"News and Views," March 1943-Dec. 1943
"Strike at Big Flats," 1946
Unit 48: "Minersville Fortnightly Nuggets," July 1945-Oct. 1945
Unit 49: "Rhythms" (1st anniversary paper), Sept. 1943
"The Dope Sheet," July 1944-March 1946
Unit 51: "The Coop Community," 1944
"Viewpoint," June 1944-April 1945
Unit 52: "Social Action News," May 1943, Aug. 1943
"Pocomoke Opinion," Sept. 1943, April 1944
School of Industrial Relations (bulletin), May-Nov. 1944 (irreg.)
Unit 53: "53", March-April 1943
Unit 55: "The Trailmaker," Dec. 1942-Nov. 1945 (irreg.)
Unit 56: "The Tide," vol. 2, No.'s 4,5
1 flier
Unit 57: "Rushmore Reflector," March 1944-Oct. 1945 (irreg.)
Unit 59: "Tap Root," Feb. 1943, April-May 1943
"The Rebel Clarion," Aug., Oct., and Dec. 1945
Unit 61: "Service," April, Oct. 1944
Unit 62: "Cheltenham News Letter," March 1943
Unit 64: "Yellowstone Builder," April 1944-May/June 1946
Unit 67: "Marsh Valley Echo," Oct./Nov. 1944, July-Oct. 1945
Unit 68: "This Issue," Dec. 1944
Unit 76: "DeTodo," July 1944
"San Dimas Rattler," Feb. 1943-Jan. 1945
Unit 81: "News of the Unit," Oct. 1944
"From Middletown," May-June 1945
Unit 84: "84 Christmas Issue," 1943
"Unit News," Nov. 1944-April 1946
Unit 87:
"Communique from Brattleboro," Feb. 1944
Unit 94: "The Irrigator," April/May 1943, Sept./Oct. 1943
"The Last Ditch," March 1945
"Paving the Paths That People Walk In" Oct. 1948
1 flyer, Oct. 1944, 1 letter, Nov. 1944
Unit 97: "BCPS Bulletin," Sept. 1945
"Dairy Diary," Oct. 1945
Units 100 & 125:
Maine "News and Views," Aug. 1945
Unit 103: "Smoke Jumper's Load Line," June 1943-Aug./Sept. 1944 (irreg.)
Unit 104: "Anniversary Report," Aug. 1944
Unit 108: "Calumet,"

July 1943-March 1945;
2 pamphlets
Unit 111: "Action,"
July 1943-June 1944
CPS GI, Nov.
1943-Dec. 1945
Unit 115: "Pulse,"
Nov. 1942

"Guinea Pig Gazette,"
May 1943
"Probe," Spring
1945-Spring 1946
"Daily Grunt," Vol. 1,
No.'s 1,2
1 bulletin; 1 flyer; 1
memo.

CLARK, HAROLD A., Collector. Miscellany, 1942-1949. 1 folder.

Archive summary: Correspondence, newsletters, and printed matter, relating to civilian public service performed by conscientious objectors in the U.S. during World War II.

COLE, BETTY. Papers, 1973-1980. 2 ms. boxes.

Coordinator, Peace Studies Program, Pacific Southwest Region, American Friends Service Committee.
Archive summary: Correspondence, bulletins, minutes, memoranda, questionnaires, curriculum material, and printed matter, relating to education for peace.

COLLINS, ERNEST, 1887- Typescript and printed poems, 1942-1955. 1 folder.

Archive summary: Relates primarily to world peace and the United Nations.

COMMITTEE ON MILITARISM IN EDUCATION.

Founded in 1925 with the aim of abolishing compulsory military training in the colleges, universities, and public high schools of the United States.
Library summary: Newsletter 1926-1927; News Bulletin Oct., Dec. 1939, Mar. June 1940; 18 pamphlets; 3 articles; report, 1939; steps to take in refusing military training; petition to President Roosevelt; 9 society publications, reprinted articles; unlisted material.

CONFERENCE FOR THE LIMITATION OF NAVAL
ARMAMENT (1927: Geneva). Mimeographed report, 1927. 1
folder.

Archive summary: Verbatim report of the second plenary
session, July 14, 1927, with declarations by the U.S. and
Japanese delegations.

CONFERENCE ON THE DISCONTINUANCE OF[iii]
NUCLEAR WEAPONS TESTS (1958: Geneva). Proceedings,
1961. 1 folder.

Archive summary: Typescript of Proceedings of several
sessions (274-276; 278-279) convened in March, 1961.

COSTE, BRUTUS, 1910-1985. Papers, 1940-1985.
2 ms. boxes.

Romanian diplomat; charge d'affaires to the United States,
1940-1941, and to Portugal, 1944-1946; secretary general,
Assembly of Captive European Nations, 1954-1965.
Archive summary: Correspondence, dispatches, memoranda,
reports, and press releases, relating to Romanian diplomacy
during World War II, discussion of Romania at the Paris
Peace Conference of 1946, postwar anticommunist movements
(especially the Truth about Romania Committee), and the
status of human rights in Romania.
Language: Romanian, English and French.

CURRAN, EDWARD LODGE, 1898-1974 Catholic Mandate
for Peace: Speech, ca. 1940-1941. 1 phonorecord.

American Roman Catholic priest; president, International
Catholic Truth Society.
Archive summary: Appeals to American Catholics to oppose
U.S. entry into World War II.

DANIELOPOL, DUMITRU. Papers, 1940-1973.
10 ms. boxes, 1 envelope.

Romanian banker; member, Romanian delegation to the Paris
Peace Conference, 1946.
Archive summary: Correspondence, writings, reports, and

28

photographs, relating to the Paris Peace Conference of 1946, the peace settlement with Romania at the end of World War II, and world politics, 1943-1973.
Language: English, Romanian and French.
Indexes: Preliminary inventory.

DARLINGTON, CHARLES F. (CHARLES FRANCIS), 1904-1986.
Papers, 1924-1985. 8 ms. boxes.

American diplomat and businessman; executive officer, Steering, Executive and Coordinating Committees, United Nations Conference on International Organization, 1945; ambassador to Gabon, 1961-1965.
Archive summary: Memoirs, speeches and writings, correspondence, memoranda, and printed matter, relating to American-Gabonese relations, the organizing conference of the United Nations, U.S. foreign trade policy, International currency exchange activities of the League of Nations, the oil industry in the Middle East, and Democratic Party politics, especially during the 1960 Presidential election.

DEKAY, JOHN WESLEY, 1874-1938. "Intellectus et Labor": Chart, 1918. 1 folder.

American businessman and author.
Archive summary: Outlines a plan to establish an International federation of workers and institutions of intellectual and manual work, contributing to the moral and social regeneration of humanity without distinction as to nationality, race, or religion among men.

DODD, NORRIS E., 1879-1968. Papers, 1900-1968.
16 ms. boxes, 3 boxes of slides, 8 scrapbooks, 3 phonorecords, 3 framed citations, 1 bust.

U.S. under secretary of agriculture, 1946-1948; director-general, United Nations Food and Agriculture Organization, 1948-1954.
Archive summary: Diaries, memoranda, reports, speeches and writings, audio-visual material, and memorabilia, relating to American and world agricultural problems.

DOLE, CHARLES FLETCHER. Associate of Stanford president David Starr Jordan who was active in American peace movement. See, AHLBORN, EMIL.

DON COSSACKS, PROVINCE OF THE.
Printed memorandum, 1919. 1 folder.

Archive summary: Relates to the Don national question and the World War I peace settlement. Presented by the delegation of the Don Republic to the Paris Peace Conference.
Language: Russian.

DRAYTON, WILLIAM A.   Papers, 1913-1946.
2 ms. boxes, 1 envelope.

American volunteer, Serbian Army; member, Serbian delegation, Paris Peace Conference; Inter-Allied commissioner, Bulgarian Atrocities Commission.
Archive summary: Correspondence, reports, memoranda, speeches and writings, and photographs, relating to Serbia during and after World War I.
Indexes: Register.

DRENIKOFF, KYRIL. Papers, 1894-1983.
153 ms. boxes, 34 oversize boxes, 3 motion picture film reels, 6 slide boxes, 22 phonotapes, 1 videotape, 106 phonorecords, memorabilia.

Counsellor to King Simeon II of Bulgaria; representative of the Bulgarian Liberation Movement to the World anticommunist League; president, Bulgarian League for Human Rights.
Archive summary: Correspondence, writings, conference proceedings, reports, bulletins, serial issues, clippings, other printed matter, photographs, maps, other pictorial materials, and memorabilia, relating to the history and culture of Bulgaria, activities of the post-World War II Bulgarian emigre community, and activities of the World anticommunist League, the Anti-Bolshevik Bloc of Nations and other anticommunist organizations. Includes diaries of Georgi Drenikov, father of K. Drenikoff, and commander of the Bulgarian Air Force during World War II.
Boxes 1-150 closed until 2016 October 6.
Language: Bulgarian.

DRESSER, ROBERT B. Papers, 1941-1967. 1 ms. box.

American lawyer.
Archive summary: Correspondence, public addresses, leaflets, and writings, relating to U.S. relations with Vietnam, Cuba, and Panama, the Korean War, communism, tax laws, civil rights, armaments, and the United Nations.
Indexes: Preliminary inventory.

DUNFORD HOUSE COBDEN MEMORIAL ASSOCIATION.
Mimeographed circular letters, 1940-1941.
1 folder.

Organization of British liberals.
Archive summary: Relates to proposed bases for peace negotiations to end World War II.

DYER, SUSAN LOUISE, 1877-1966. Papers, 1895-1965. 9 ms. boxes, 1 scrapbook, 10 envelopes, 1 oversize folder, 1 phonotape, 1 gilded metal buddha.

Lifelong friend of Herbert and Lou Henry Hoover; American Red Cross worker in France, 1918-1919.
Archive summary: Correspondence, diary, scrapbooks, memorabilia, clippings, photographs, tape recording, and printed matter, relating to Herbert Hoover, Lou Henry Hoover, Stanford University, the Hoover Institution, the Girl Scouts, and the American Red Cross in France during World War I.

ECKHARDT, WILLIAM, 1918- Writings, 1965-1981.
1 ms. box.

Director of the Peace Research Laboratory in St. Louis, Missouri.
Archive summary: Journal articles dealing with the psychological, ideological, and social sources of forms of aggressiveness (e.g., militarism) and non-aggressiveness (e.g., peace).

EUROPEAN SUBJECT COLLECTION, 1889-1984.
7 ms. boxes.

Archive Summary: Pamphlets, leaflets, serial issues, posters, proclamations, certificates, reports, and correspondence, relating to miscellaneous aspects of twentieth-century European history, and especially to the socialist movement in Europe between the two world wars.
NOTES: Section on European socialist parties includes leaflets on "Antikriegmuseum" in Germany, 1930-31. From Scandinavian countries there are serial issues relating to politics, socialism, and the peace movement in Scandanavia.
Language: German, Dutch, Norwegian and other European languages.
Indexes: Register.

EVANS, ARTHUR MAYBURY, 1874-1967. Miscellaneous papers, 1913-1967.
1 ms. box.

American journalist.
Archive summary: News stories, clippings, speeches and writings, post cards, and memorabilia, relating to the Paris Peace Conference of 1919, and to miscellaneous political events.

FACKERT, HAROLD E., Collector. Miscellany, n.d. 1 ms. box.

Archive summary: Pamphlets, clippings, and other published materials relating to pacifism.

FELLOWSHIP OF RECONCILIATION[ii,iii] (F.O.R.), U.S. BRANCH. Records, 1942-1946. 20 ms boxes.

British pacifist society established in 1914; American branch founded in 1915.
Archive summary: Correspondence, reports, and memoranda pertaining to the FR's role as a defender of conscientious objectors and to antiwar activities during World War II.
Library summary: Membership list, Nov. 1925; 30 pamphlets; 1 folder of books and pamphlets, 1945; 36 society publications, incl. leaflets, broadsides; unlisted material.
Indexes: Preliminary inventory.

FIELD, HERBERT HAVILAND, 1868-1921.

Papers, 1919. 1 folder.

Typed transcript.
Member of the U.S. delegation to the Paris Peace Conference of 1919.
Archive summary: Diary and reports, relating to political and economic conditions in Bavaria, January-March, 1919.

FIELITZ, AXEL VON. Über die Bedeutung des Haager Werkes: Holograph memorandum, 1915. 1 folder.

Archive summary: Relates to a proposal to end World War I through reconvening the Hague International Peace Conference.
Language: German.

FRANK, COLMAN D. Miscellaneous papers, 1918-1919. 1 folder, 1 envelope.

Major, U.S. Army, during World War I; member, U.S. Section, Permanent International Armistice Commission.
Archive summary: Guide for interrogation of German prisoners; military map of Germany and route book; memoir (typewritten), entitled **Inside the Armistice** Commission; and photographs of Allied members of the Permanent International Armistice Commission, and of U.S. military activities in World War I.

FRANK, KARL BOROMAUS, 1893-1969 Papers, 1937-1961. 10 ms. boxes, 1 envelope, 7 microfilm reels. Entire collection also available on original negative microfilm copy.

German psychologist; socialist and anti-Nazi leader.
Archive summary: Writings, correspondence, clippings, printed matter, and photographs, relating to the communist, socialist, and anti-Nazi movements in Germany, post-World War II reconstruction in Germany, and political psychology.
Language: German and English.
Indexes: Register.

FREE, ARTHUR M., Collector.
Photographs, 1914-1918. 8 envelopes.

Archive summary: Depicts German troops and war scenes on the Eastern and Western fronts during World War I, and scenes of the negotiation of the Treaty of Brest-Litovsk, 1918. Captions in German.
Language: German.

FRENCH DETERRENCE: An Assessment: Video program, 1983.
1 video cassette.

Archive summary: Relates to French nuclear weapons and their impact on International arms control negotiations. Includes interviews with Foreign Minister Claude Cheysson of France and Henry A. Kissinger. Produced by the Press and Information Service of the French Embassy in the United States for American audiences.

FRIED, ALFRED HERMANN, 1864-1921. Papers, 1914-1921.
5 ms. boxes.

A native of Austria, Alfred Fried was a jurist who became a dedicated pacifist during the early years of this century. Along with Bertha von Suttner, his colleague and mentor, he founded the German Peace Society (Deutsche Friedensgesellschaft) in 1892 and served as editor of its major publication, Monatliche Friedenkorrespondenz, (Monthly Peace Correspondence). He later edited several International peace journals, such as Blätter für Internationale Verstaendigung und zwischenstaaliche Organisation, Papers for International Understanding and Interstate Organization, and The Peace Watch). He achieved international recognition in 1911 when he was awarded the Nobel Peace Prize.
Archive summary: Original diaries; correspondence (1910-1914); writings (1914-1919); and scrapbook (1900-1914). Printed materials are housed in the library.
Library summary: The library houses over 2,520 items and consists mainly of books, pamphlets, annuals, and files of serials. The materials pertain to such subjects as International law, nationalism, Internationalism, and militarism, particularly as they relate to the Great Powers in the pre-war years. Included in the collection are parts of the library of Baroness Bertha von Suttner, whose writings on world politics and peace influenced not only Fried but also a whole generation of pacifists. Suttner is perhaps best known for her work, Die Waffen Nieder! (1889), which was one of the most important antiwar novels of the period. Dr. Fried's printed war diary in 18 volumes is also included in this section.

FRIENDS COMMITTEE ON NATIONAL LEGISLATION[ii,iii] (U.S.)
Issuances, 1983-1985. 3 v. in 2 ms. boxes.

Lobbying organization established in 1943 and affiliated with the Society of Friends.
Archive summary: Newsletters, reports, minutes, testimony, statements, and letters of advocacy, relating to efforts of the committee to influence Congressional legislation in the areas of peace, disarmament, military policy, civil rights, social policy, and the promotion of International understanding.
Library summary: 4 books; 6 society publications; 5 pamphlets; unlisted material.
See also, FRIENDS, SOCIETY OF...

FRIENDS, SOCIETY OF. VARIOUS SECTIONS.

Family of Quaker organizations largely concerned with promoting peace and social reconciliation through public service.
Library summary: 26 pamphlets; L'Essor Dev. 1947; International Service, April 1922; India and Pakistan, Annual Report, 1951; Friends Ambulance Unit; A Year in Honan, Oct. 1946; Report April-Nov. 1915, Dec. 1945; Annual Report 1939-1943, 1940-1941, 1946. Friends' Peace Committee; 9 pamphlets; 2 society publications.
See also, AMERICAN FRIENDS SERVICE COMMITTEE, and FRIENDS COMMITTEE ON NATIONAL LEGISLATION.

FURLONG, CHARLES WELLINGTON, 1874-1967. Papers, 1917-1963. 1 map, 10 ms. boxes, 9 envelopes.

A delegate to the Paris Peace Conference of 1919; member of Tacna-Arica Commission, 1926.
Archive summary: Correspondence, memoranda, reports, writings, clippings, maps, and photographs, relating to Woodrow Wilson, the Paris Peace Conference, military, political, and economic conditions in the Balkans (particularly relating to Fiume and Montenegro), the Tacna-Arica dispute between Peru and Chile, and the work of the Tacna-Arica Plebiscitary Commission, 1925-1926.
Indexes: Register.

GAY, EDWIN FRANCIS, 1867-1946. Papers, 1917-1927.

6 ms. boxes, 1 roll of charts.

American economist; director, U.S. Central Bureau of Planning and Statistics, 1918-1919.
Archive summary: Correspondence, diary, reports, memoranda, and writings, relating to U.S. economic mobilization and government control of the economy during World War I, and to activities of the Central Bureau of Planning and Statistics, War Industries Board, War Trade Board, Shipping Board, and Commercial Economy Board, and to the U.S. delegation at the Paris Peace Conference.

GERMANY. AUSWAERTIGES AMT. GESCHÄFTSTELLE FÜR DIE FRIEDENSVERHANDLUNGEN.
Typescript extracts from memoranda, n.d. 1 folder.

German Office for Peace Negotiations.
Archive summary: Relates to negotiations concerning the eastern boundaries of Germany at the Paris Peace Conference. Includes translation made by Alma Luckau. Language: German.

GIBSON, HUGH, 1883-1954. Papers, 1900-1957.
126 ms. boxes, 27 oversize boxes, 22 envelopes, 2 microfilm reels, 1 phonorecord.

American diplomat; ambassador to Poland, 1919-1924; ambassador to Switzerland, 1924-1927; ambassador to Belgium and Luxemburg, 1927-1933 and 1937-1938; ambassador to Brazil, 1933-1937.
Archive summary: Diaries, writings, correspondence, reports, minutes of meetings, photographs, and printed matter, relating to U.S. foreign relations, international disarmament, the League of Nations, and relief work in Europe during World Wars I and II.
Diaries also available on microfilm.

GRAHAM, MALBONE, 1898- Papers, 1914-1956.
16 ms. boxes, 2 card file boxes.

American political scientist.
Archive summary: Pamphlets, bulletins, writings, memoranda, and clippings, relating to the League of Nations, and to political conditions and diplomatic relations in Finland, the Baltic States, and Eastern Europe, from the Russian

GRIN, J. Testimonial, 1913.

Archive summary: A tribute to the Austrian pacificist Bertha von Suttner entitled, "Prolong Opgedragen aan de Vrede-Vorstin de Hoog Welgeboren Vrouwe Baronesse von Suttner."
Language: Dutch.

GROSE, ADA MORSE, 1874- Papers, 1914-1918.
1 ms. box, 1 envelope, 1 oversize box.

American pacifist; secretary to David Starr Jordan, president of Stanford University; participant, Henry Ford Peace Conference and Neutral Conference for Continuous Mediation. Stockholm, 1916.
Archive summary: Correspondence, memoranda, reports, passports, clippings, handwritten notes, certificate of citizen registration, peace badges, and photographs, relating to the peace movement during World War I.

GROSSMANN, KURT RICHARD, 1897-1972. Papers, 1926-1973.
53 ms. boxes, 8 scrapbooks.

Journalist and president of the German League for Human Rights, 1926-1933.
Archive summary: Materials on two Nobel peace laureates, Carl von Ossietzky (1935) and Willy Brandt (1971).
Language: English and German.

GRUBBS, FRANK LESLIE, 1931- Collector. Collection, 1917-1974. 1 folder, 10 microfilm reels.

Archive summary: Microfilm copies of correspondence, minutes, and printed matter, from various sources, relating to activities of the American Alliance for Labor and Democracy and the People's Council of America in competing for labor support on the question of U.S. participation in World War I. Used as research material for the book by F. L. Grubbs, The Struggle for Labor Loyalty (1968).
NOTE: Included in the collection are letters of Jane Addams,

Emily C. Balch, and Morris Hillquit.
Indexes: Preliminary inventory.
See also, ADDAMS, JANE, BALCH, EMILY GREENE.

HASL, FRANZ JOSEPH. Miscellaneous Papers, 1916-1919.
1/2 ms. box.

Austrian writer and pacifist.
Archive summary: Papers include a memorandum entitled "Universal Peace" and a letter to Woodrow Wilson dated 1919.

HERMAN, RAPHAEL. Letter, 1918, to Woodrow Wilson. 1 folder. Typed transcript.

Archive summary: Relates to proposals by R. Herman for the basis of a peace settlement to end World War I, especially regarding territorial questions.

HERRON, GEORGE DAVIS., 1862-1925. Papers, 1916-1927.
30 ms. boxes, 16 volumes, 4 scrapbooks, 2 microfilm reels.

At one time a radical Christian Socialist clergyman, Herron later abandoned socialist politics in favor of pacifism. At the Paris Peace Conference he was the unofficial adviser to President Woodrow Wilson.
Archive summary: Correspondence, interviews, lectures, essays, and clippings, relating to the League of Nations, territorial questions, prisoners of war, and other political and economic issues at the Paris Peace Conference.
Indexes: Preliminary inventory.

HERTER, CHRISTIAN ARCHIBALD, 1895-1966.
Miscellaneous Papers, 1921. 1 folder.

American statesman; assistant to Secretary of Commerce Herbert Hoover, 1919-1924; secretary of state, 1959-1961.
Archive summary: Correspondence with Manley O. Hudson and Arthur Sweetser, officials of the League of Nations, relating to accomplishments of the League of Nations and to prospects of the League for maintenance of peace and resolution of International disputes in the future.

HOLLINGSWORTH, SIDNEY PIERCE. Papers, 1941-1969.
2 ms. boxes.

American writer.
Archive summary: writings, clippings, and miscellanea, relating to historical trends in the twentieth century, public relations and the social order, the League of Nations and World Court, and a variety of other historical themes.

HOOVER, HENRY, 1788-1868. Journals, 1862-1868. 1 oversize box.

Farmer from Wayne County, Indiana; distant relative of Herbert Hoover.
Archive summary: Includes observations on the course of the American Civil War (1861-1865), pacifism, the Society of Friends and the Methodist Episcopal Church, and reminiscences on Hoover family history.

HOOVER, HERBERT, 1874-1964. Papers, 1895-1987. 367 ms. boxes, 6 microfilm reels, 130 motion picture film reels, 1 video cassette, 1 oversize box, 91 envelopes, 2 oversize folders, 31 phonorecords, 36 phonotapes, memorabilia.

President of the U.S., 1929-1933.
Archive Summary: Correspondence, speeches and writings, appointment calendars, printed matter, photographs, motion picture film, and sound recordings, relating to twentieth-century American politics, and to relief administration in World Wars I and II. Indexes: Register.

INTERNATIONAL COMMITTEE FOR IMMEDIATE MEDIATION, 1916.
Records.

Organization created by the Henry Ford Peace Expedition and the Neutral Conference for Continuous Mediation.
Archive summary: Reports and minutes of meetings of the ICIM during World War I.
Language: English, German, and Norwegian.

INTERNATIONAL CONGRESS OF WOMEN. (The Hague, 1915); INTERNATIONAL CONGRESS OF WOMEN. (Zurich

1919). See, WOMEN'S INTERNATIONAL LEAGUE FOR PEACE AND FREEDOM. 1ST AND 2ND CONGRESSES.

INTERNATIONAL PEACE CONFERENCE. Photographs, 1899-1907. (also known as Hague Peace Conference) 2 framed Photographs.

Archive summary: Depicts delegates to the first and second Hague Peace Conference, 1899-1907. Includes identification chart for the second photograph.
Language: Undetermined.

INTERNATIONAL STUDIES CONFERENCE (1932: Milan). Mimeographed report, 1932. 1 v. (1 folder)

Conference held under the auspices of the International Institute of Intellectual Cooperation of the League of Nations.
Archive summary: Report of the fifth session.

JANSEN, B. DOUGLASS, Collector. Collection, 1961-1966. 1 folder.

Archive summary: Press releases, statements, and speech transcripts, relating to proposals for disarmament and a nuclear test ban. Issued by officials and agencies of various governments, especially the U.S. Arms Control and Disarmament Agency, and the Soviet Embassy in the United States.

JOHNSON, DOUGLAS. Letter, 1918, to J. Spencer Smith. 1 folder. Typed transcript.

Chief, Division of Boundary Geography, U.S. Delegation to the Paris Peace Conference, 1919.
Archive summary: Relates to territorial settlements at the Paris Peace Conference.

JORDAN, DAVID STARR, 1851-1931. Papers,* 1794-1950. 88 ms. boxes, 1 oversize box, 5 scrapbooks, 5 envelopes, memorabilia. *Also available on microfilm at Stanford

University's Green Library.

American educator and pacifist; president, Stanford University, 1891-1913; chancellor, Stanford University, 1913-1916. Jordan's antiwar book, War and Waste, was published in 1913. After leaving Stanford, he continued his antiwar activities, principally as the director of the American Peace Society.

Archive summary: Correspondence, writings, pamphlets, leaflets, clippings, and photographs, relating to pacifism and the movement for world peace, disarmament, international relations, U.S. neutrality in World War I, U.S. foreign and domestic policy, civil liberties in the U.S., problems of minorities in the U.S., Stanford University, and personal and family matters.

NOTE: Dr. Jordan's extensive correspondence files contain letters exchanged with renowned figures of the peace movement, scientists, and statesmen throughout the world. Among the correspondents are the following: Jane Addams (1912-1929), Emily G. Balch (1916-1928), Bureau of International Peace (1914), Henry Ford (1915-1923), Alfred H. Fried (1910-1921), Herbert Clark Hoover (1906-1929), Peace and Arbitration Society of Buffalo N.Y. (1911-1914), Ezra Pound (1928-1930), Theodore Roosevelt (1901-1917), Rosika Schwimmer (1914), Upton Sinclair (1915-1918), William Howard Taft (1910-1918), Woodrow Wilson (1913-1920), and Women's International League for Peace and Freedom (1922-1931). Indexes: Register.

Library summary: There are some 500 books and pamphlets on peace and internationalism and materials relating to various peace societies, among them, the Women's International League for Peace and Freedom. Included in this collection are the reports of the first meetings of the League held in The Hague (1915).

In the Reference room of Stanford University's Green Library there is a guide to the microfilm edition of the David Starr Jordan papers, 1861-1964. Ralph W. Hansen, project director; Patricia J. Palmer, editor; Connie Stein, editorial assistant. A project of the Stanford University Archives in the Stanford University Libraries. Sponsored by the National Historical Publications Commission. [Stanford, 196-?] 31 p. port. 23 cm.

JUENGER, ERNST, 1895-

Der Friede: ein Wort an die Jugend Europas, ein Wort an die Jugend der Welt: typescript essay, 1944. 1 v.
Archive summary: Relates to post-World War II reconstruction.
Language: German.

KARMIN, OTTO, 1882-1920. Miscellaneous Papers, 1902-1918.
1 folder.

Austrian historian.
Archive summary: Letters by Friedrich Wilhelm Foerster, Petr Kropotkin, Franz Oppenheimer, Elisée Reclus, and Hans Vaihinger, relating to anarchism, pacifism, and various aspects of the international situation; and transcript of a lecture by Tomas Masaryk, relating to Czechoslovak nationalism.
Language: French and German.

KASLAS, BRONIS J., 1910- Papers, 1918-1974.
4 ms. boxes.

Lithuanian historian.
Archive summary: Writings and rare printed matter, relating to Eastern European politics, the Russian occupation of Lithuania, Lithuanians in foreign countries, the Baltic States, Poland, and the Paris Peace Conference of 1946.
Indexes: Preliminary inventory.

KERTESZ, STEPHEN D. (STEPHEN DENIS), 1904-1986. Papers, 1932-1986. 180 ms.boxes, 1 oversize folder, 1 album box, 1 microfilm reel, 1 phonotape, 2 phonotape cassettes.

Hungarian diplomat; secretary-general, Hungarian delegation, Paris Peace Conference, 1946; subsequently political scientist in the United States.
Archive summary: Correspondence, speeches and writings, memoranda, reports, clippings, and other printed matter, relating to the politics, economy and diplomacy of Hungary, minority problems involving Hungary or Hungarians, the Paris Peace Conference of 1946, modern diplomatic history, and international relations.
Language: English and Hungarian.
Indexes: Preliminary inventory.

KITTREDGE, TRACY BARRETT, 1891-1957. Papers, 1910-1957.
51 ms. boxes, 6 envelopes.

A Captain in the U.S. Navy and member of the Commission for Relief in Belgium, Kittredge participated in several diplomatic missions. Among other things, his Papers relate to the Commission for Relief in Belgium, 1914-1924 and the Paris

Peace Conference, 1919.

KLEINHANS, ELEANOR M., Collector. Collection, 1972-1987.
1 ms. box.

Archive summary: Consists of clippings and other printed materials about the peace movement during the Vietnam War era, (1960s-1970s).

KOESTNER, NICOLAI. Miscellaneous Papers, 1920-1921.
1 folder.

Estonian consul in New York City.
Archive summary: writings, press summaries, and memoranda, relating to diplomatic recognition of Estonia by the U.S. and other countries, and to the admission of Estonia to the League of Nations.
Language: English and French.

KRUPENSKII, ALEKSANDR NIKOLAEVICH, 1861-1939.
Papers, 1918-1935. 9 ms. boxes.

Marshal of Bessarabian nobility; president, Bessarabian Provincial Zemstvo; Bessarabian delegate to the Paris Peace Conference, 1919.
Archive summary: Correspondence, memoranda, lists, extracts, summaries, reports, appeals, projects, protocols, press analyses, maps, forms, drafts, clippings, newspaper issues, journals, bulletins, and pamphlets, relating to the Bessarabian question; relations between Russia, Romania and Bessarabia; the occupation and annexation of Bessarabia by Romania, 1918; and to the Paris Peace Conference.
Language: Russian, French and Romanian.
Indexes: Register.

LANSING, ROBERT, 1864-1928. Miscellaneous Papers, 1916-1927. 1 folder. Photocopy. Originals in Library of Congress.

Secretary of state of the U.S., 1915-1920.
Archive summary: Diaries, correspondence, and memoranda, relating to U.S. foreign policy during World War I and to the Paris Peace Conference in 1919.

LATIN AMERICAN SUBJECT COLLECTION, 1914-1990. 10 ms. boxes, 1 oversize box, 7 slide boxes, 2 oversize folders, 16 phonorecords, 3 videocassettes.

Archive summary: Reports, correspondence, position papers, bulletins, serial issues, newsletters, flyers, campaign material, circulars, speeches, clippings, minutes resolutions, charts, photographs, and miscellaneous publications relating to the history and political conditions in various Latin American countries, including Argentina, Bolivia, Chile, Costa Rica, El Salvador, and Honduras. Specific topics covered include the Bolivian revolution of 1946; the Chilean military coup of September, 1973; guerrilla movements in Central America; and the peace initiatives aimed at ending civil strife in Central America during the 1980s.

LEAGUE OF NATIONS. Slides, n.d. 1 box.

Archive summary: Depicts officials and activities of the League of Nations.
Inventory.

LEAGUE OF NATIONS. HIGH COMMISSIONER, FREE CITY OF DANZIG.

High Commissioner's decision in the Danzig-Gdingen conflict: mimeographed decision, n.d. 1 v. (in 1 folder)
Archive summary: Relates to the dispute between Danzig and Poland regarding the use of the port of Danzig.

LEAGUE OF NATIONS.[ii,iii] **OFFICIAL PUBLICATIONS, 1920-1946.**

The Hoover Institution served as a deposit library for all official publications of the League, which was established in the wake of World War I in order to preserve world peace. The organization came into being at a time when the tide of antiwar sentiment had peaked in Europe and the Americas. Although it survived for nearly 26 years, it was widely viewed as an ineffectual organization -- especially as it failed to prevent the outbreak of World War II in 1939. Despite its shortcomings, however, the idea of the League lived on, and the organization was superseded by the creation of the United Nations in 1945.
Library summary: Approximately 6,600 items, including 9

books; 117 serials; 5 pamphlets; reports (April 1934, Oct. 1945); reviews (1926, 1930, 1935); and protocols and resolutions (1924).

LEAGUE OF WOMEN VOTERS.

Organization founded in 1920 to foster education in citizenship; to promote forms of public discussion; and propose legislative reforms. At various times in its history the LWV has renounced war as an instrument of national policy.
Library summary: 1 book; News Letter 10 & 20 June 1940; press releases; annual convention proceedings 1921-1923; Trends news service 1945-1948; 46 misc. publications; 4 society publications; 5 pamphlets; unlisted material; National Planning Association; 54 books; 2 reports; 85 pamphlets; 4 "Planning Methods" series; 7 society publications.

LLOYD GEORGE, DAVID, 1ST EARL, 1863-1945. Typescript essay, 1934. 1 folder.

British statesman.
Archive summary: Relates to the Geneva Disarmament Conference and to prospects for world disarmament.

LOCKLEY, FRED, Collector. Collection, 1931-1936.
1 ms. box.

Archive summary: Letters, notices, clippings, and mimeographed material, relating to pacifism, disarmament, and the American pacifist leader Sydney Strong.

LOGAN, JAMES ADDISON, JR., 1879-1930. Papers, 1913-1924.
5 ms. boxes, 18 v.

American banker; colonel, U.S. Army; U.S. representative, Supreme Economic Council, during World War I; unofficial U.S. representative, Reparations Commission, 1919-1924.
Archive summary: Correspondence, reports, and memoranda, relating to the U.S. war effort in World War I, conditions of prisoners of war, the Paris Peace Conference, postwar reconstruction in Europe, and war reparations.
Indexes: Preliminary inventory.

LONDON. NAVAL CONFERENCE, 1930. Miscellaneous Records, 1930.
1 ms. box.

International conference on naval armament limitations.
Archive summary: Minutes of meetings, reports of committees, and rosters of delegates.
Language: French and English.

LOUCHEUR, LOUIS, 1872-1931. Papers, 1916-1931.
13 ms. boxes, 1 envelope.

French industrialist, statesman, and diplomat.
Archive summary: Correspondence, speeches, notes, reports, and photographs, relating to industry in Russia during World War I, inter-Allied diplomacy during World War I, war reparations, and postwar French and international politics.
Indexes: Preliminary inventory.
Language: French.

MCCORMICK, VANCE C., 1872-1946. Diaries, 1917-1919.
1/2 ms. box.

McCormick was one of the American delegates sent to the Inter-Allied Conference, 1917, and an adviser to Woodrow Wilson at the Paris Peace Conference, 1919.
Archive summary: Papers relate to inter-Allied diplomacy and the Paris Peace Conference.

MALIK, CHARLES HABIB, 1906-
"The United Nations as an ideological battleground, typescript speech, 1971. Conference on the United Nations at 25: Performance and Prospects (1971: Hoover Institution on War, Revolution and Peace) 22 p.
1 folder. Photocopy.

Lebanese diplomat; president, United Nations General Assembly, 1958-1959.
Archive summary: Delivered at the Conference on the United Nations at 25: Performance and Prospect, held at the Hoover Institution on War, Revolution and Peace.

MANUILA, SABIN, 1894-1964. Papers, 1940-1975.

23 ms. boxes, 1 oversize box.

Romanian statistician and politician.
Correspondence, memoranda, reports, speeches and writings, clippings, printed matter, and other material, relating to political events in Romania, and Romanian anticommunist emigre movements.
Language: Romanian and English.

MARX, GUIDO HUGO, 1871-1949.
"War and the Conscientious Objector," typescript of speech, 1936.

Professor Marx taught Machine Design at Stanford University.
Archive summary: Transcript of his speech which relates to the pacifist movement in the United States.

MASLAND, JOHN WESLEY, JR., 1912-1968. Papers, 1945.
21 ms. boxes, 1 envelope.

A staff member of the International Secretariat of the United Nations.
Archive summary: Reports, minutes of meetings, directories, notes and printed matter relating to the United Nations Conference on International Organization held in San Francisco in 1945.

MAVERICK, LEWIS A. Papers, 1914-1940.
4 ms. boxes.

American pacifist.
Archive summary: personal Papers relating to the Henry Ford Peace Expedition (1915), and the Neutral Conference for Continuous Mediation and International Committee for Immediate Mediation (1916).

MEHRING, FRANZ, 1846-1919. Miscellaneous Papers, 1914-1918.
1 folder.

German socialist leader.
Archive summary: Writings and correspondence, relating to

political conditions in Germany and to the peace movement during World War I.
Language: German.

MILLER, DAVID HUNTER, 1875-1961.

Library summary: The library holds his 21 volume work entitled My Diary at the Conference of Paris, with Documents.

MILLIS, WALTER, 1899-1968.
ABOLITION OF WAR: Mimeographed study, 1962.
1 folder.

Archive summary: Relates to prospects for peace through international disarmament. Written by W. Millis and James Real. Subsequently published.

MOHSELL, IRMELA, Collector. Collection, 1982-1985.
1 folder.

Archive summary: Clippings, pamphlets, and other printed matter, relating to peace movements and education for peace in East and West Germany and in Norway.
Language: German and Norwegian.

MONETARY AND ECONOMIC CONFERENCE (1933: LONDON) Miscellaneous Records, 1933.
1 ms. box.

Archive summary: Proposals, memoranda, and resolutions, relating to international cooperation in commerical and financial policy.

MORAN, HUGH ANDERSON, 1881-1977 Papers, 1916-1933.
2 ms. boxes.

American clergyman; Young Men's Christian Association worker in Siberia and China, 1909-1918.
Archive summary: Correspondence, writings, clippings, maps, posters, and photographs, relating to the Russian Civil War,

political and economic conditions in Siberia and Manchuria, and relief work in Siberia and Manchuria, especially in the prisoner of war camps, during the Russian Civil War.
Indexes: Preliminary inventory.

MORSE, JOHN H. Papers, 1957-1973. 4 ms. boxes.

U.S. deputy assistant secretary of defense for European and NATO affairs, 1970-1973.
Archive summary: Correspondence, speeches and writings, memoranda, studies, and printed matter, relating to nuclear warfare strategy, questions of nuclear arms testing and disarmament, the positioning of nuclear missiles in Europe as a part of the North Atlantic Treaty Organization alliance, and the development of the neutron bomb.

MUNRO, DANA CARLETON, 1866-1933. Papers, 1908-1923.
4 ms. boxes, 1 microfilm reel.

U.S. Inquiry investigator, Paris Peace Conference, 1919; research assistant, Committee on Public Information, 1917-1918.
Archive summary: Reports, correspondence, and leaflets relating to political and economic conditions in Turkey, Zionism, relief work and the conduct of German occupying forces in Belgium during World War I, U.S. neutrality in World War I, war propaganda, and proposals for world peace.

NATIONAL COUNCIL FOR THE PREVENTION OF[ii,iii]
WAR. WESTERN OFFICE, SAN FRANCISCO, 1921-1954.
Records, 1921-1943.
3.5 ms. boxes.

American pacifist organization.
Archive summary: Leaflets, notes, reports, and other Papers of this pacificist organization. Most of the collection relates to peace, disarmament, U.S. neutralitiy in World War II, anti-conscription, and anti-military training in educational institutions.
Library summary: National Council for Prevention of War (until 1922 National Council for Reduction of Armaments); 1 book; Washington, D.C. office, 6 books; Western office, San Francisco, 2 books; Educational Series No.'s 1-3; 30 society publications; 22 pamphlets; unlisted material.

NATIONAL PEACE COUNCIL[ii,iii] (London, England)

Federation of various kinds of British organizations concerned with peace and the development of international cooperation. Founded in 1904, the NPC has sought to influence public opinion on peace issues through education and the dissemination of information.
Library summary: 24 books; 1 book of treaty texts, declarations on World War II reconstruction, world affairs; 3 books, Commission on East-West Relations 1 government document; 1 flyer.

NATIONAL REPUBLIC MAGAZINE. Records, 1920-1960. 826 ms. boxes.

American anticommunist magazine.
Archive summary: Clippings, pamphlets, reports, indices, notes, bulletins, lettergrams, weekly letters, and photographs primarily concerned with communist, fascist, and pacifist movements in the United States and the Soviet Union. Indexes: Register.

NATIONAL SECURITY LEAGUE[ii,iii]

Founded in New York City in 1914, the NSL was a right-wing organization that opposed American neutrality in WWI and promoted patriotism and militarism in the United States.
Library summary: Approximately 200 pamphlets, hand bills, rebase sheets, charts and maps, including the following: 9 books; 2 books, Committee on Patriotism through Education "HWL" No's. 1-13,16,18,19; 6 reports; study of the U.S. Constitution; 69 U.S. Propaganda publications; Bulletin, Vols. 1/4; 40 Society Publications; 24 pamphlets; circular letter; proceedings and delegates of Congress on Constructive Patriotism, Correspondence Course on Patriotism, 1-13; Committee Minutes; Hearings 1-30, except 26 and 29; 15 posters; 146 leaflets; 4 charts; 2 mailing folders; 6 cards, applications; 4 news clippings; 1 address; 1 article; unlisted material; National Service Board for Religious Objectors; 6 books; 5 society publications; and 1 pamphlet.

NEW LEFT COLLECTION, 1964-1988.

Between 1969 and 1973, the collection development of the N.L.C. at the Hoover Institution was directed by Dr. Edward

J. Baccioco, author of The American New Left: Reform to Revolution, 1956-1970 (Hoover Institution, 1974). The collection itself is divided into two groups. One consists mainly of serial publications which are housed in the Library. As a rule, ephemeral items (including leaflets, newsletters, clippings, and miscellaneous issues of newpapers and periodicals) are held as a special collection in the Archives.
Archive summary: 87 ms. boxes, 1 microfilm reel, 3 phonorecords. Booklets, leaflets, reports, and clippings, relating to the purposes, tactics, and activities of various New Left and right-wing groups, draft resistance, student disorders, and the anti-Vietnam War movement.
Indexes: Registers.
Library summary: New Left material housed in the Library is listed in the card catalog under a number of different headings: Armed Forces – Political activity; College students – political activity; Communism - 1945 - ; Labor and Laboring Classes - Political activity; Radicalism; Right and Left (Political Science); Riots; Students - Political Activity; Trade Unions - Political Activity, etc. Among the serial publications found here is the Bell and Howell/University Microfilm International Underground Newspaper Microfilm Collection. Over 728 alternative newspapers titles published in the United States and Europe between 1963-1987 are represented in this collection of 492 reels.
See also, STANFORD DRAFT COUNSELING OFFICE, STUDENTS FOR A DEMOCRATIC SOCIETY.

NEW YORK PEACE SOCIETY,[ii,iii] 1906-1940.

Established in 1906, the NYPS promoted the establishment of permanent international courts, the progressive development of international law, and the limitation of armaments world wide.
Library summary: 3 books, including an address delivered by Elihu Root; unlisted material.

NEWCOMBE, HANNA. Writings, 1968-1983.
1 ms. box.

Canadian social scientist; co-editor, Peace Research Abstracts Journal, 1962- .
Archive summary: Studies, reprints, and journal articles, relating to peace, international tension measurement, International organization, and voting patterns in the United Nations. Includes writings of Alan G. Newcombe and others.

NOWAK, BOHDAN, 1900- Vox mortuum: Printed Portfolio of Drawings, ca. 1930'S. 1 envelope.

Polish artist.
Archive summary: Artwork that depicts the horrors of war.
Language: French.

OLIVEREAU, LOUISE, DEFENDANT. Typescript trial transcript, 1917. 1 ms. box.

American anarchist.
Archive summary: Relates to the trial of L. Olivereau in U.S. District Court, Western District of Washington, Northern Division, on charges of inciting insubordination and obstructing recruitment in the U.S. Army during World War I. Includes text of indictment.

OSUSKY, STEPAN, 1889-1973. Papers, 1910-1981.
1 v., 102 ms. boxes, 2 card file drawers, 1 cylinder, 5 envelopes, 1 oversize box.

Czechoslovakian diplomat; ambassador to Great Britain, 1918-1920; ambassador to France, 1920-1940; minister of state, Czechoslovakian Government-in-Exile, 1940-1943.
Archive summary: Correspondence, memoranda, reports, clippings, printed matter, memorabilia, and photographs, relating to Czechoslovakian politics and diplomacy, and European diplomatic relations between the two world wars.
Language: English, French, Czech and Slovak.

PACIFIST RESEARCH BUREAU[iii] (Philadelphia).

Library summary: 17 books; 15 pamphlets, Series I-VII; 2 society publications; 1 pamphlet; 1 radio program; unlisted material.

PARIS CONFERENCE TO CONSIDER THE DRAFT TREATIES OF PEACE WITH ITALY, RUMANIA, BULGARIA, HUNGARY AND FINLAND (1946).
Mimeographed Miscellaneous Records, 1946.
1 ms. box.

Archive summary: Transcripts of proceedings, summaries,

speeches, and agenda, relating to the peace settlement at the end of World War II.
Language: English, French and Russian.

PARIS PEACE CONFERENCE, 1919.[iii] Records, 1919-1921.
87 linear feet.

The Library and Archives have an extensive collection of mimeographed, printed, and printed but unpublished collection of documents that include the following: (a) Minutes of the plenary sessions of the Paris Peace Conference and the sessions of Powers with Special Interests. (b) Minutes of the meetings of the Supreme Council (including the Council of Ten, the Council of Five, and the Council of Heads of Delegations — although the early meetings for the latter are missing). (c) Minutes of the meetings of the Council of Ministers for Foreign Affairs (January 10-20, 1920), of the Inter-Allied Conference of Prime Ministers (January 16-20, 1920), and of the Conference of Ambassadors (January 26, 1920-January 12, 1921). (d) S.H. and E.S.H. Bulletins compiled respectively by the American Commission to Negotiate Peace and the United States Embassy, Paris. These cover the period 1919 and 1921 and contain materials relating to the activities of the Supreme Council and the Council of Ambassadors.
(e) Minutes and/or reports of 36 commissions and committees of the Peace Conference, e.g., Commission on Belgian and Danish Affairs, Commission on Baltic Affairs, etc.
See also, **PEACE SUBJECT COLLECTION**

PARIS PEACE CONFERENCE (1919-1920) COMMISSION ON BALTIC AFFAIRS. Minutes, 1919. Typed transcript.
1 folder.

Archive summary: Relates to aspects of the World War I peace settlement regarding the Baltic States. Includes some proceedings of the commission.
Language: Mainly French.

PARIS PEACE CONFERENCE, 1919. A Statement to the Peace Conference: Typescript, 1919.
1 folder.

Archive summary: Opposes the creation of a Jewish state in Palestine. Presented to the Paris Peace Conference by a group of Jewish Americans, March 4, 1919.

PARIS PEACE CONFERENCE, 1919. U.S. DIVISION OF TERRITORIAL, ECONOMIC AND POLITICAL INTELLIGENCE. Miscellaneous Records, 1917-1918.
7 ms. boxes, 3 card file boxes.

Organization created to provide U.S. delegation with background information on countries attending the Paris Peace Conference; known as the Inquiry.
Archive summary: Documents primarily relate to political and economic conditions in the Ottoman Empire and Latin America, proposals for new boundaries in Asia Minor, creation of an independent Armenia, and boundary disputes in South America.

PARK, ALICE, 1861-1961. Papers, 1883-1957.
30 ms. boxes, 3 envelopes.

American pacifist, feminist, and socialist who was a member of the Henry Ford Peace Ship Expedition, 1915.
Archive summary: Diaries, correspondence, pamphlets, press clippings, and leaflets relating to pacifism and the peace movement, the Ford Peace Ship Expedition, feminism, socialism, the labor movement, prison reform, child labor legislation, civil liberties, and a variety of other reform movements in the United States.
Indexes: Register.

PASTUHOV, VLADIMIR D., 1898- Papers, 1927-1938.
58 ms. boxes, 2 rolls, 1 envelope, 3 oversize boxes.

Secretary, League of Nations Commission of Enquiry in Manchuria, 1931-1934.
Archive summary: Correspondence, memoranda, reports, interviews, maps, photographs, and printed matter, relating to the investigation of the Manchurian incident of 1931.
Language: Chinese, English, French, and Russian.
Indexes: Preliminary inventory.

PEACE POSTERS, 1918-1988. (Poster collection)
807 posters on peace interspersed among the country collections found in the Archive's Poster Collection.

Archive summary: Over 32 countries are represented, with the largest number originating from the following: United States (327); United Kingdom (89); Germany (88); Soviet Union (55);

and France (42).

PEACE SUBJECT COLLECTION, 1891-1982.
17 ms. boxes, 4 phonotape cassettes boxes; published and unpublished sources (including audio-visual material) on peace.

Archive summary: Pamphlets, clippings, leaflets, letters, memoranda, circulars, reports, and bulletins, relating to pacifism, disarmament, international law, the Paris Peace Conference of 1919, the League of Nations and other actual or proposed international organizations, and various proposed plans to ensure peace. Specific contents include pamphlets, leaflets, letters, memoranda, circulars, reports, and bulletins published between 1891 and 1982, relating to pacifism, conventional and nuclear disarmament, the League of Nations, and various plans to ensure world peace; pamphlets published between 1900 and 1930 on international law, the League of Nations, questions of war and peace, territorial disputes, and reparations; clippings, miscellanea, and a photograph relating to Cyrus H. Street, editor of The United Nations bulletin, published in Berkeley, California, 1908-1911, and a copy of the first issue of the bulletin (November, 1908); newspaper clippings from various French Papers and the Paris edition of the London Daily Mail relating to the Paris Peace Conference (1919-1921); clippings relating to Louis Botha's prayer for world peace written during the Paris Peace Conference; clippings from American newspapers relating to the Washington D.C. Conference on the Limitation of Armaments (1921-1922); four cassette tapes of speeches and songs from the October 1981 demonstation against nuclear armaments, held in Bonn, West Germany.
Language: Various languages, including French, German, Italian, and English.
Indexes: Register.
See also, LEAGUE OF NATIONS, PARIS PEACE CONFERENCE, 1919

PENNINGTON, LEVI TALBOTT, 1875- Correspondence, 1928-1962, with HERBERT HOOVER.
Photocopy. 1 folder.

President, Pacific College, Newberg, Oregon.
Archive summary: Relates to Pacific College, disarmament, the National Committee on Food for the Small Democracies, and the Boys' Clubs of America.

PEOPLE'S COUNCIL OF AMERICA.[ii,iii]

Library summary: 3 books; press matter; 1 pamphlet; 4 society publications; minutes; 2 folders of misc.; The People's Council for Democracy and Peace; 1 envelope of clippings; 6 society publications, from Northern and Southern California branches; 17 leaflets; personal and circular letters; 9 misc. Items; 1 env., from Alice Park collection; press matter; 3 pamphlets; 1 address; minutes from 1st executive meeting, Sept. 1917; unlisted material.
See Also, ALICE PARK.

PETRESCU-COMNEN, NICOLAE, 1881-1958. Papers, 1917-1958.
22 ms. boxes.

Romanian diplomat; delegate to the League of Nations, 1923-1928 and 1938; ambassador to Germany, 1927-1929 and 1932; minister of foreign affairs, 1938.
Archive summary: Correspondence, writings, reports, diplomatic dispatches, clippings, and serial issues, relating to Romanian foreign relations, especially with Germany, Switzerland, and the Vatican; the League of Nations; World War II refugees and relief work; and postwar Romanian emigre life.
Language: Romanian, French, Italian, German and English.

PIIP, ANTONIUS. Mimeographed Writings, 1920-1932.
1 folder.

Prime minister of Estonia, 1920-1921.
Archive summary: Relates to the independence of Latvia, diplomatic recognition of Estonia, Estonian membership in the League of Nations, and relations between Estonia and the Soviet Union.
Language: English and French.

POLAND. AMBASADA (Great Britain) Records, 1918-1945.
133 ms. boxes.

Polish Embassy in Great Britain.
Archive summary: Correspondence, memoranda, reports, financial records, studies, conference proceedings, and printed matter, relating to Anglo-Polish relations, especially relations between Great Britain and the Polish Government-in-Exile in

London during World War II; Anglo-Polish trade; Polish foreign policy and participation in the League of Nations during the interwar period; conditions in Poland during World War II; and wartime activities of the Polish Government-in-Exile.

POLAND. MINISTERSTWO PRAC KONGRESOWYCH.
Miscellaneous records, 1940-1944. 15 ms. boxes.

Ministry of Preparatory Work Concerning the Peace Conference, Polish Government-in-Exile (London).
Archive summary: Essays, bulletins, reports, and studies relating to Poland's boundary disputes following World War I; events and conditions in Poland under German and Soviet occupations during World War II and questions involving Poland at the general peace conference that was expected to follow the victory of the Allies; Polish-Soviet relations; communism in Poland; and twentieth century Polish domestic and foreign affairs.
Indexes: Preliminary inventory.

POLAND. MINISTERSTWO PRAC KONGRESOWYCH. RADA MORSKA.
Mimeographed miscellaneous records, 1942-1944. 1 ms. box.

Marine Council of the Ministry of Preparatory Work Concerning the Peace Conference. Polish Government-in-Exile (London).
Archive summary: Reports, studies, statistical data and statutes relating to Polish shipping boundaries and territorial disputes with the Soviet Union during World War II. Materials were issued, in part, by the Department of Marine Affairs of the Ministry of Industry, Commerce and Transportation of the Polish Government-in-Exile.

POLAND. "SOLIDARITY" COLLECTION, 1976-1991. Papers being processed in 1990-1991. Over 150 ms boxes.

Archive summary: Leaflets, bulletins and other serial publications (approximately 1,200 titles). Some 25 titles issued by the "Wolnosc i Pokoj" (Freedom and Peace) movement cover a variety of themes, including draft resistance efforts and pacifist activities of anti-establishment youth in Poland during the late 1980s and early 1990s.

POPOVSKII, MARK ALEKSANDROVICH, Collector.
Collection, 1919-1977. 16 microfilm reels.

Archive summary: Reminiscences, reports, correspondence, and other writings of members of the Tolstoyan Pacifist movement in the Soviet Union, 1918-1970s.
Indexes: Preliminary Inventory.

PRAVDA. Typescript translations of excerpts, n.d.
1 folder.

Russian Bolshevik newspaper.
Archive summary: Relates to the socialist peace conference in Stockholm, and to the suppression of the Bolsheviks during the July days. Excerpts are dated July-August 1917. Includes a false satirical issue of Pravda, 1980, prepared by anticommunists.
Language: German.

PUSTA, KAAREL ROBERT, 1883- Papers, 1918-1964.
20 ms. boxes.

Estonian diplomat; foreign minister of Estonia, 1924-1925.
Archive summary: Correspondence, speeches and writings, memoranda, reports, printed matter, and photographs, relating to Estonian politics and diplomacy, Soviet-Baltic States relations, the League of Nations, international law, and Estonian emigre politics. Language: Estonian, French and English.
Indexes: Preliminary inventory.

QUIDDE, LUDWIG, 1858-1941. "Deutschland nach dem Kriege: Ein Programm für dauernden Frieden" (Germany after the War: A Program for Lasting Peace): typescript, n.d.
1 folder.

German historian and politician who was a peace a activist during the first decades of the twentieth century. Member of the Council of the International Peace Bureau (Berne), leader of the World Peace Congress at Glasgow in 1901, and president of the German Peace Society for 15 years.
Archive summary: Typescript (mimeographed) of his peace proposal.

RADISICS, ELEMER, 1884- Papers, 1920-1964.
5 ms. boxes, 1 oversize box.

Hungarian attorney, statesman, diplomat, and journalist; chief, Historical Department, Ministry of Foreign Affairs; editor, Budapesti Hirlap; member, Secretariat, League of Nations, 1931-1940.
Archive summary: Correspondence, reports, diplomatic dispatches, military and historical studies, clippings, and printed matter, relating to Hungarian history, politics, and government, the Danube Valley, the Hungarian Revolution of 1956, World War II military campaigns, world politics, Palestinian history, and Jewish-Arab relations.

REED, HOWARD A. (HOWARD ALEXANDER), 1920- Papers, 1951-1983. 50 ms. boxes.

American historian and educator; director, Institute of International and Intercultural Studies, University of Connecticut, 1967-1971.
Archive summary: Correspondence, memoranda, reports, studies, notes, curricular material, conference papers and proceedings, and printed matter, relating to the promotion of international education in the United States; Middle Eastern area studies, and especially Turkish studies, in the United States; and activities of the American Friends Service Committee and other organizations in promoting education for peace and international exchange programs for students.

REQUIN, EDOUARD JEAN, 1879-1953. Papers, 1915-1940.
4 ms. boxes.

General, French Army; liaison officer between French and American General Staffs, 1918; commanding general, French 4th Army, 1939-1940.
Archive summary: Correspondence, military orders, memoranda, and writings, relating to Allied military operations in World War I, particularly Franco-American military cooperation; to proposals for a treaty of mutual assistance under auspices of the League of Nations, 1922- 1923; and to operations of the French 4th Army, May-June 1940. Language: French.

RICHARDSON, GRACE, Collector. Miscellany, 1919.
1 folder.

Archive summary: Printed matter, clippings, and badges, relating to the League to Enforce Peace; the American Red Cross; a 1919 reception for President Woodrow Wilson in Omaha, Nebraska; and women's suffrage in Nebraska. Indexes: Preliminary inventory.

RIEFFEL, ARISTIDE, 1859-1941. Papers, 1890-1941.
36 ms. boxes.

French journalist and pacifist.
Archive summary: Correspondence, writings, pamphlets, and photographs that pertain to various themes, including, international arbitration, pacifism, Alfred Nobel and the Nobel Peace Prize.

RIGA, TREATY OF, 1920.

Typescript translation of preliminary peace treaty and armistice, 1920. 1 folder.
Archive summary: Treaty between Poland and Russia, signed at Riga, October 11, 1920, halting the Russo-Polish War.

RINGLAND, ARTHUR C. Papers, 1921-1960.
1 folder.

American Relief Administration worker in Czechoslovakia, 1921-1922.
Archive summary: Memoranda and printed matter, relating to League of Nations cooperation with American Relief Administration activities in Russia, the attitude of Aleksandr Kerensky in 1921 toward American Relief Administration activities in Russia, and subsequent Soviet attitudes toward American Relief Administration activities in Russia.

RITTER, GERHARD, 1888-1967. Writings, 1947.
1 folder.

German historian.
Archive summary: writings, including Kirche und Internationale Ordnung, relating to the ecumenical movement and world peace, and Die Falschung des Deutschen Geschichtbildes im Hitlerreich, relating to the falsification of the German historical image in the Hitler Reich.

Language: German.

ROBINSON, HENRY MAURIS, 1868- Papers, 1917-1936.
34 ms. boxes, 1 envelope.

American lawyer and banker; U.S. representative to various international economic conferences.
Archive summary: Correspondence, speeches and writings, reports, minutes of meetings, memoranda, conference documents, and printed matter, relating to the U.S. Council of National Defense during World War I, the Paris Peace Conference, the Allied Supreme Economic Council, the Dawes and Young Committees on Reparations, and the International Economic Conference of 1927.
Indexes: Register.

ROTHWELL, CHARLES EASTON, 1902-1987. Papers, 1924-1988.
24 ms. boxes, 1 oversize box.

American educator and historian; United States Department of State official (1941-1945); secretary general, U.S. delegation to the United Nations, 1946; director, Hoover Institution (1952-1959); president, Mills College (1959-1967).
Archive summary: Writings, correspondence, memoranda, reports, printed matter, photographs, and sound recordings relating to the United Nations; American foreign policy (especially in Asia); the study of international relations; and to the administration of the Hoover Institution, Stanford University, Mills College, the Asia Foundation, and the National War College.
Preliminary inventory.

RUSSIA. POSOL'STVO (FRANCE). Records, 1916-1924.
37 ms. boxes.

Russian Embassy in France.
Archive summary: Correspondence, reports, and memoranda relating to relations between France and the Russian Provisional Government, the Russian Revolution, counter-revolutionary movements, the Paris Peace Conference, and Russian emigres after the revolution.
Indexes: Register.
Language: Russian and French.

SAPON'KO, ANGEL OSIPOVICH, 1876-1944. Papers, 1900-1944. 11 ms. boxes.

Russian sociologist, political scientist, pacifist, and Chief of the Stenographic and Records Division of the Duma.
Archive summary: Correspondence, reports, essays, studies, printed materials, and photographs that relate to Christianity, disarmament, pacifism, religion, science, and other subjects. In Russian. Includes papers of Zoia G. Brandt, his assistant, and materials pertaining to A.V. Kossiakovskaia, exiled fiancee of Grand Duke Mikhail Aleksandrovich.
Indexes: Preliminary Inventory.
Language: Russian.

SARLES, RUTH, 1906- A History of America First: typescript history, 1942. 2 V.

Archive summary: Relates to the America First Committee, isolationist lobby in the U.S. during World War II.

SCHMIDT, FRIEDA, 1894-. Papers, 1914-1945. 1 ms. box.

German pacifist.
Archive summary: Personal diaries and collection of publications on pacifism and social conditions in Germany during the Nazi era.
Language: German.

SCHUDER, KURT. Typescript Writings, 1948. 1 folder.

Archive summary: Relates to world peace and German-American relations.
Language: German.

SCHWIMMER, ROSIKA, 1877-1948. Papers, 1914-1937. 2 ms. boxes, 1 envelope.

Hungarian pacifist and feminist. In 1915 Schwimmer was one of the envoys sent through Europe by the International Congress of Women, which was then headed by the social reformer, Jane Addams.
Archive summary: Correspondence, petitions, clippings, and

photographs relating to her participation in various pacifist causes, including her efforts to secure the assistance of the United States government in negotiating an end to World War I between 1914 and 1917, WWI peace movements, the Henry Ford Peace Expedition, International Congress of Women, 1915-1951, and the World Peace Prize awarded to her in 1937.
NOTE: Autograph letters signed by a number of eminent politicians, writers, and social reformers, notably Jane Addams, Gabriel D'Annunzio, John Galsworthy, Herbert Hoover, Aleksandr Kerenskii, Cecil Rhodes, T.G. Masaryk, Kaiser Wilhelm II, and Woodrow Wilson.
Indexes: Preliminary Inventory.

SHANGHAI PEACE DELEGATION. Printed declaration, 1948.
1 folder.

Archive summary: Relates to a Shanghai delegation sent to the Nationalist government at Nanking to urge a peaceful conclusion to the Chinese Civil War. Includes translation (typewritten).
Language: Chinese with English translation.

SHAW, JOHN PUTNAM, 1923-1974. Papers, 1948-1973.
1 ms. box.

American diplomat; director, U.S. Office of Disarmament and Arms Control, 1968-1973.
Archive summary: Writings, personnel records, correspondence, memoranda, and press releases, relating to Soviet-American disarmament negotiations and to world communism.

SHISHMANIAN, JOHN AMAR, 1882-1945. Papers, 1903-1945.
1 ms. box, 3 envelopes.

Captain, French Foreign Legion during World War I.
Archive summary: Correspondence, printed matter, photographs, and memorabilia, relating to the Armenian-Turkish conflict at the end of World War I, and to the Armenian question at the Paris Peace Conference.
Indexes: Preliminary inventory.
Language: English, French and Armenian.

SLOSSON, PRESTON W. (PRESTON WILLIAM), 1892-
Typescript letter, 1924, to E. D. ADAMS. 1 folder.

Staff member, U.S. delegation, Paris Peace Conference, 1919.
Archive summary: Relates to the existence of records of the proceedings of the Paris Peace Conference.

SPITZER, ROBERT R., 1922- Papers, 1954-1989.
91 ms. boxes, 5 oversize boxes, 2 motion picture film reels.

American businessman and educator; coordinator, Food for Peace Program, U.S. Agency for International Development, 1975-1976.
Archive summary: Correspondence, reports, minutes, drafts of writings, printed matter, and audio-visual material, relating to Food for Peace, world food supply and agricultural production, and Wisconsin and U.S. politics, especially the 1968 and 1972 presidential campaigns of Richard M. Nixon.
Indexes: Preliminary inventory.

STANFORD, BARBARA DODDS, 1943–. Papers, 1968-1981.
1/2 ms. box.

American educator and author.
Archive summary: Writings, course outlines, and other educational materials relating to peace and conflict resolution.

STANFORD DRAFT COUNSELING OFFICE. Collection, 1967-1973. 3 ms. boxes.

Archive summary: Newsletters, handbooks, leaflets, and ephemeral publications on military conscription in the United States issued by government agencies, legal organizations, and political action groups. (Materials were collected by the S.D.C.O.)
Indexes: Preliminary inventory.
See also, **NEW LEFT COLLECTION, 1964-1988.**

STOWELL, ELLERY CORY, 1875-1958. Papers, 1909-1920.
1 ms. box.

American legal scholar.

Archive summary: Correspondence, writings, printed matter, and clippings, relating to the London Naval Conference of 1909, and various proposals for international limitation of armaments.

STREET, CYRUS H. See, PEACE SUBJECT COLLECTION.

STRONG, SYDNEY. Mimeographed newsletters, 1932-1933.
1 folder.

Observer at the Geneva Disarmament Conference.
Archive summary: Relates to the conference and to the world disarmament movement.

STUDENTS FOR A DEMOCRATIC SOCIETY.

American student protest group active in the 1960s. The SDS initially campaigned for nuclear disarmament, but later became involved in other antiwar activities, including organizing draft resistance during the American phase of the Vietnam War.
Library summary: 8 books; investigations of hearings; Papers, plus index (microfilm) 1958-1970.
See also, NEW LEFT COLLECTION, 1964-1988.

SUMANS, VILIS, 1887-1948. Papers, 1925-1948.
1 ms. box, 1 envelope.

Latvian diplomat and statesman; director of administrative and political departments, Ministry of Foreign Affairs, 1919-1924; delegate to the League of Nations Assemblies, 1922-1930; minister to Italy, 1924-1926; to France, 1926-1934; and to Spain and Portugal, 1928-1933.
Archive summary: Correspondence, memoranda, bulletins, press excerpts, clippings, photographs, memorabilia, and other materials, relating to Latvian foreign relations, 1925-1948.
Languages: Latvian, French and German.

SUTTNER, BERTHA VON, former secretary to Alfred Nobel and author of Die Waffen Nieder! (Lay Down Your Arms!). See, FRIED, ALFRED HERMANN.

SWORAKOWSKI, WITOLD S. Papers, 1921-1972.
3 ms. boxes, 4 microfilm reels, 1 phonotape.

Polish-American historian; assistant and associate director, Hoover Institution on War, Revolution and Peace, 1956-1970. Archive summary: Statistics, writings, translations, maps, and printed matter, relating to the ethnography of Upper Silesia in 1910; Polish boundary questions, 1918-1945; the Paris Peace Conference of 1919; communism in Eastern Europe after World War II; and the shipment of the 1917 abdication proclamation of Tsar Nicholas II.
Language: Mainly in Polish and English.

TA CHUNG CULTURAL COOPERATION ASSOCIATION. Struggle for Peace and Democracy in the Northeast: typescript translation of report, 1947. 1 folder.

Archive summary: Relates to military activities of the Chinese Communist Party in Manchuria against the Japanese during World War II and against the Kuomintang. Language: Chinese (English translation).

THOENNINGS, JOHAN. "The Golden Book: A Document for the British, French, American, and German Nations," 1939. 1 folder.

Archive summary: Relates to a plan for the assurance of world peace.

TITTLE, WALTER, 1883- Hand-drawn portraits, 1922.
1 oversize box.

American artist.
Archive summary: Depicts American, British, Japanese, French, Italian, Belgian, and Chinese delegates to the Washington Conference on the Limitation of Armament, 1921-1922. Portraits are autographed by their subjects.
Indexes: Inventory.

TITULESCU, NICOLAE, 1882-1941. Papers, 1923-1938.
17 ms. boxes, 1 envelope, 4 microfilm reels.

Romanian statesman and diplomat; minister of finance,

1920-1922; ambassador to Great Britain and delegate to the League of Nations, 1922-1927; minister of foreign affairs, 1927-1928 and 1932-1936.
Archive summary: Diaries, correspondence, memoranda, reports, writings, clippings, and printed matter, relating to Romanian politics and diplomacy, and to Romanian-Soviet negotiations, 1931-1932. In French and Romanian. Box 17 closed. Eligible to be opened upon the death of Georges Anastasiu.
May be used only if name of user and copy of any publication based on the collection are made available to Mme M. Y. Antoniade.
Indexes: Register.
Language: French, Russian and Romanian.

TRUE, ARNOLD, 1901-1979. Papers being processed in 1990-1991.

Retired Navy Rear Admiral who won the Navy Cross, the Distinguished Service Medal and the Purple Heart in the battles of the Coral Sea and Midway during World War II. After his retirement, True became an academic and was placed under government surveillance in the 1960s for his anti-Vietnam war activities.
Archive summary: Correspondence, writings and publications relating primarily to True's military career and participation in the anti-Vietnam war movement in the United States.

UNITED NATIONS ASSOCIATION OF THE UNITED STATES OF AMERICA. SAN FRANCISCO CHAPTER. Records, 1945-1970.
37 ms. boxes, 2 oversize boxes, 74 motion picture reels.

Private American organization supporting the United Nations.
Archive summary: Correspondence, memoranda, financial records, pamphlets, and other assorted printed matter that pertain to the activities of the United Nations, world politics, and international human rights.

UNITED NATIONS.[iii] CONFERENCE ON INTERNATIONAL ORGANIZATION (1945: San Francisco). Sound recordings of proceedings, 1945. 146 phonorecords.

Founding conference of the United Nations.
Archive summary: Recordings made by the National

Broadcasting Company.

UNITED NATIONS. PREPARATORY COMMISSION OF THE UNITED NATIONS. Records, 1945. 1 microfilm reel.

Archive summary: Microfilm of Commission's work relating to the founding of the United Nations.

UNITED STATES. ARMY. BOARD OF INQUIRY (CAMP LEWIS, WASHINGTON) Typed transcripts of hearings, 1918. 1 ms. box.

Archive summary: Relates to appeals of men inducted into the U.S. Army to be granted conscientious objector status.

UNITED STATES. DEPT. OF STATE.[iii] Miscellaneous records, 1942-1967. 1 ms. box.

Archive summary: Microfiche copies of reports, memoranda, and correspondence, 1967, relating to the Israeli naval and air attack on the U.S.S. "Liberty" on 8 June 1967, issued by various offices of the Department of State, and publicly released under the Freedom of Information Act; and mimeographed reports, 1942-1943, relating to the imposition of international sanctions against aggressor nations, and to the effects of League of Nations sanctions against Italy in 1935-1936.

UNITED STATES. SELECTIVE SERVICE SYSTEM. Mimeographed report, 1944. 1 folder.

Archive summary: Relates to U.S. government policy regarding conscientious objectors and to criticisms of this policy made by the National Committee on Conscientious Objectors.

VANDERHOOF, FRANK E.
"Vanderhoof 13-point Peace Plan to Eliminate Future Wars," mimeographed outline, 1943. 1 folder.

Archive summary: Typescript of outline of Vanderhoof's

proposal for world peace.

**VAN KEUREN, ALEXANDER HAMILTON, 1881-1966.
Papers, 1899-1962.** 8 ms. boxes, 2 envelopes.

Rear Admiral in U.S. Navy who served as a technical adviser at the London Naval Conferene, 1930 and the Geneva Disarmament Conference, 1932.
Archive summary: Documents relating to these conferences.
Register.

VOICE OF PEACE. Sound recorded message.

American religious pacifist organization.
Appeals to American women to pray for peace. Includes a recording of the song "Ava Maria" sung by Wilma Reynolds.

WAR RESISTERS' INTERNATIONAL.[ii,iii] **ARCHIVES OF THE WAR RESISTERS' INTERNATIONAL, 1921-1974.** [Microform].

Established in 1921 as a society which sought to unite all those who refused to support any war. Its basic statement of purpose holds that war is a crime against humanity. Members are expected to to oppose all wars and "strive for the removal of all causes of war." Today, the WRI is a non-aligned peace organization with sections in 17 countries.
War Resister. War Resistance. Bulletin (War Resisters' International) Newsletter (War Resisters' International) Hassocks, Sussex, England: Harvester Press, 1977. 103 microfiches ; 11x15 cm..
NOTES: Contents: Card 1. Introd. and contents -- Cards 2-25. Pamphlets 1921- 1974 -- Cards 26-62. Bulletin 1923-1974 [title changed to The War Resister in 1926, and to War Resistance in 1962] -- Cards 63-65. Annual appeals and related documents -- Cards 66-76. Minutes of Council meetings and minutes of International Council meetings 1926-1974 -- Cards 77-90. Minutes of Executive Committee meetings and supplementary Papers 1955-1974 -- Card 91. Secretary's report 1947-1974 -- Cards 92-100. Newsletter 1962-1974 -- Card 101. Press releases 1964-1974 -- Cards 102-103. Training in non-violence 1968- 1973.
Library summary: 15 books; 4 books (German); 1 book (French); 1 book (Spanish); 17 pamphlets; International Conference 1925, 1928; War Resister League (American branch of WRI) 7 books; 3 pamphlets; International Conference 1946.

WARDEN, A.A. Writings, CA. 1924-1929.
1 folder.

British physician and pacifist.
Archive summary: Typescript of Warden's writings relating to the medical profession's responsibilities and relationship to the pacifist movment.

WEGERER, ALFRED VON, 1880-1945. Writings, 1941.
1 folder.

German historian.
Archive summary: Typewritten study of his entitled, "From War to Peace," which is about the causes of World War II and the prospects for peace. There is also a photocopy of a memorandum (typewritten in German) relating to the proposed establishment of an Academy on War and Peace associated with the Hoover Institution.
Language: English and German.

WHITE, HENRY, 1850-1927. Miscellaneous Papers, 1919.
1 folder. Photocopy. Originals in Library of Congress.

American diplomat; member, American delegation, Paris Peace Conference, 1918-1919.
Archive summary: Memoranda and resolutions, relating to the work of the Paris Peace Conference. A Statement to the Peace Conference typescript, 1919 that opposes the creation of a Jewish state in Palestine. Presented to the Paris Peace Conference by a group of Jewish Americans, March 4, 1919.

WILLIAMS, MARY WILHELMINE, 1878-1944. Papers, 1911-1943.
1.5 linear ft.

Stanford University Libraries, special collections M047
Mary Wilhelmine Williams was a professor of history, author, and authority on Latin America and inter-American relations.
Archive summary: Letters, diaries, clippings, and manuscripts pertaining to Dr. Williams' interest in the Kensington Stone, education in Latin America, the Women's International League for Peace and Freedom, and Dom Pedro of Brazil. Includes manuscripts of Dr. Williams' writings as well as reviews. Gift of Dr. Mary Williams, 1944.

Indexes: Unpublished guide available.

WILLIS, BAILEY, 1857-1949. Papers, 1916-1943.
2 ms. boxes.

American geologist; chief, Latin American Division, the Inquiry, 1918.
Archive summary: Studies, correspondence, and photographs, relating to activities of Stanford University and former Stanford students during World War I, the Tacna-Arica boundary dispute, European topography, and submarine warfare logistics during World War II.
Indexes: Preliminary inventory.

WILSON, HOWARD E. (HOWARD EUGENE), 1901-1966. Papers, 1919-1966. 37 ms. boxes.

American educator; assistant director, Division of Education, and executive associate in charge of education, Carnegie Endowment for International Peace, 1945-1953.
Archive summary: Speeches and writings, correspondence, memoranda, reports, printed matter, and photographs, relating to education in the United States and Turkey, international education, and activities promoting education undertaken by the United Nations Educational, Scientific and Cultural Organization, its Preparatory Commission, and the Carnegie Endowment for International Peace.

WISSMANN, HELLMUTH, B. 1884- Typescript Writings, 1939-1947. 1 folder.

Archive summary: Typescript on national socialism in Germany, the role of propaganda, post-World War II reparations, and plans for world peace.
Language: German.

WOLFE, BERTRAM DAVID, 1896-1977. Papers, 1903-1989. 192 ms. boxes, 2 card file boxes, 1 oversize box, 19 envelopes, 6 microfilm reels, 3 videotape cassettes, 12 phonotapes, 2 phonotape cassettes.

An antiwar activist during World War I, Wolfe remained throughout his life an opponent of war. He was also one of

the founders of the U.S. Communist Party, of which he was a member until 1929. After leaving the party he became an historian, writer, and political analyst of communism. He is perhaps best known as the author of Three Who Made a Revolution (1948), The Fabulous Life of Diego Rivera (1963), and his posthumously published autobiography A Life in Two Centuries (1981).
Archive Summary: Writings, correspondence, notes, memoranda, clippings, other printed matter, photographs, and drawings, relating to Marxist doctrine, the international communist movement, communism in the Soviet Union and in the U.S., literature and art in the Soviet Union and in Mexico, and the Mexican artist Diego Rivera. Includes papers of Ella Wolfe, wife of B. D. Wolfe.
NOTES: Correspondence relating to peace includes the following: America First Committee; Society of Friends; American Friends Service Committee (1943-1973).
Indexes: Register.

WOMAN'S PEACE PARTY.[ii,iii] The Collected Records of the Woman's Peace Party, 1914-1920 [Microform]. Wilmington, DE: Scholarly Resources Inc., 1988. 23 microfilm reels ; 35 mm.

Stanford University Libraries, Microtext MFILM N.S. 10084. Scholarly Resources, inc. Swarthmore College. Peace Collection.
NOTES: Published in cooperation with the Swarthmore College Peace Collection, Swarthmore, PA.
"Consists of records of the Woman's Peace Party that were collected by the Swarthmore College Peace Collection in the 1930s"--Introd. Contents: reel 1-7. Series A. Historical records -- reel 8-19. Series B1. Correspondence, National Office, Chicago, 1915-1919 -- reel 20-23. Correspondence, New York Branch, 1915-1919.

WOMEN'S INTERNATIONAL LEAGUE[iii] FOR PEACE AND FREEDOM. Papers, 1915-1978; A Guide to the Microfilm Edition, edited by Mitchell F. Ducey. Sanford, N.C.: Microfilming Corporation of America, 1983.
130 p.; 28 cm.

Stanford University Libraries, Microtext JX1965.W465 1983 Ducey, Mitchell F., Women's International League for Peace and Freedom.
NOTES: Includes bibliographical references. Purchased as a cooperative acquisition by Stanford and the University of

California. The material listed in this guide is located at Stanford.

WOMEN'S INTERNATIONAL LEAGUE FOR PEACE AND FREEDOM. Papers [Microform]: 1915-1978. Sanford, North Carolina: Microfilming Corporation of America, 1983. 114 microfilm reels ; 4 in., 35 mm.

Stanford University Libraries, Microtext MFILM N.S. 3318 Women's International League for Peace and Freedom.
NOTES: Purchased as a cooperative acquisition by Stanford and the University of California.
For contents consult the guide to the microfilm edition (JX1965.W465 1983) located in the Reference Department and Current Periodicals and Microtext Division.
Library summary: 13 books; 2 books, German; 1 book, French; 7 flyers; 15 vols, Int'l Congresses 1-18 (except 8, 14, 17) 1915-1971.
Languages: German, French, English

WOMEN'S INTERNATIONAL LEAGUE FOR PEACE AND FREEDOM.
1ST CONGRESS, THE HAGUE, 1915. Memorandum, 1915. 1 folder.

Archive summary: Typescript regarding the founding of the WILPP (later known and the Women's International League for Peace and Freedom), and to its efforts to end WWI.

WOMEN'S INTERNATIONAL LEAGUE FOR PEACE AND FREEDOM.
2ND CONGRESS, ZURICH, 1919. Mimeographed Resolutions, 1919. 1 folder.

Archive summary: Mimeographed typescript that relates to the peace settlement of World War I, the League of Nations, and the rights of women.

WOMEN'S INTERNATIONAL LEAGUE FOR PEACE AND FREEDOM.
U.S. SECTION. The Women's International League for Peace and Freedom, United States Section, 1919-1959 [microform] / editor, Eleanor M. Barr. Records of the Women's International League for Peace and Freedom-- United States Section. [Wilmington, DE]: Scholarly Resources Inc., [1980-1987] 97 microfilm reels; 35 mm.

Stanford University Libraries, Microtext MFILM N.S. 10085
Barr, Eleanor. Scholarly Resources, inc. Swarthmore College.
Peace Collection.
NOTES: "Published in cooperation with the Swarthmore
College Peace Collection, Swarthmore, PA." Publisher's Note
cites as: "Records of the Women's International League for
Peace and Freedom--United States Section, 1919-1959." "The
Swarthmore College Peace Collection is the official repository
for the records of the United States Section of the Women's
International League for Peace and Freedom
(WILPF)."–Introd. Contents: reel 1-37. Series A. Historical
records -- reel 38-92. Series C. Correspondence -- reel 93-97.
Series E. Serial publications. For contents consult user's guide:
Records of the Women's Internationl League for Peace and
Freedom, United States Section, 1919-1959, guide to the
Scholarly Resources microfilm edition (Z6464.Z9R4 1988),
located in Current Periodicals/Microtext.

WORLD PEACE COUNCIL[iii] (Helsinki)

The WPC campaigns for the the prevention of war, peaceful
co-existence and global disarmament. It advocates the
settlement of disputes through negotiation. It also opposes
colonialism and racial discrimination in the belief that these
practices pose a threat to international peace.
Library summary: 54 books, including documents, reports of
members, Papers, 1 book, Czechoslovakian; 3 books, French; 2
books, German; 6 books, Russian; 2 books, Spanish; list of
members, 1977-1980; programme of action, 1979, 1983; 8
anticommunist pamphlets; speech of Fidel Castro; World
Peace Foundation; 53 books, including documents; 1 book of
conference Papers; pamphlet series, 1941- ; pamphlets, vols.
1-12 ; pamphlets, Jan. 1935- ; pamphlets, 1933- ; studies in
citizen participation in international relations, volumes
1-2,4-6; charters of the United Nations, plus commentary;
Foreign Policy Reports 1-3; index to League of Nations'
economic and financial documents; text of Peace Conferences
1899 and 1907; program, list of members, 1915; 12 pamphlets; 1
society publication.
Languages: Czech, English, French, German, Russian, Spanish.

WORLD WITHOUT WAR COUNCIL[ii] COLLECTION,
1948-1984.
11 ms. boxes.

Group that looks for ways to resolve international conflicts
without violence. In addition to organizing conferences,
education and training programs, the WWWC publishes a

variety of materials related to war and peace that are primarily aimed at influencing U.S. State Department policies.
Archive summary: Serial issues, bulletins, and newsletters, relating to peace, pacifism, disarmament, American foreign policy, world affairs, and the Vietnamese War. Collected by the World without War Council of Northern California. Indexes: Register.

ZILBERMAN, BELLA N. Papers, 1924-1959.
1/2 ms. box.

American peace advocate.
Archive summary: Writings, letters, and printed matter concerned with Zilberman's plans to bring about world peace.

ZORN, PHILIPP KARL LUDWIG, 1850-1928. See, PEACE SUBJECT COLLECTION.

PART II: ORGANIZATIONS

This section lists the names of national and international organizations (i.e., associations, societies, etc.) in the library whose files contain assorted publications relating to peace. The reader should bear in mind that, while these document groups vary in size and scope, they are considerably less extensive than those collections represented in Part I.

All-America Anti-Imperialist League
All-India Preparatory Peace Committee
Allied and Associated Powers
America First Committee[i]
American Arbitration Association
American Association for Adult Education
American Bar Association. Committee on War Work
American Committee for Struggle Against War
American Committee for the Outlawry of War
American Committee on War Finance
American Congress for Peace and Democracy
American Foundation
American Friends Fellowship Council[i]
American Friends Peace Conference
American Friends Reconstruction Unit
American Friends Service Committee[i,iii]
American Jewish Committee
American League Against War and Fascism[i,iii]
American League to Limit Armaments
American Legion
American Neutral Conference Committee
American Peace and Arbitration League[iii]
American Peace Award

American Peace Congress
American Peace Crusade[iii]
American Peace Mobilization[iii]
American Peace Society[i,iii]
American Peace Terms Committee
American School Citizenship League
American School Peace League
American Society for Judicial Settlement of International Disputes[iii]
American Union Against Militarism[i,iii]
Americans for Peace
Anglican Pacifist Fellowship
Anti-Conscription Committee
Anti-Enlistment League
Anti "Preparedness" Committee
Arms Control and Disarmament Agency[iii]
Arms of Friendship, Inc.
Arunachal Mission[iii]
Association for Peace Education
Association to Abolish War
Better World Club
Better World Fund
Bibliotheque Pacifiste Internationale
Brethren Service Commission. Brethren Service Committee
Buffalo Peace and Arbitration Society[iii]
Bureau International Permanent de la Paix
Bureau of the World Peace Mission
California State Conference Against War and Fascism
Campaign for Nuclear Disarmament[i,iii]
Canadian Disarmament Information Service[iii]
Canadian Institute for International Peace and Security[iii]
Canadian Peace Congress[iii]
Canadian Peace Research Institute[iii]
Carnegie Endowment for International Peace[i,iii]

Catholic Association for International Peace[iii]
Catholic Association for International Peace. Committee on Ethics.
Catholic Pacifists' Association
Center for Research on World Political Institutions
Center for the Study of Armament and Disarmament
Center for the Study of Democratic Institutions[iii]
Center for War/Peace Studies[iii]
Central Board for Conscientious Objectors
Central Committee for Conscientious Objectors
Central Organization for a Durable Peace
Centre Interdisciplinaire de Recherches sur la Paix et d'Etudes Strategiques[iii]
Chicago Committee to Oppose Peacetime Conscription
Chicago Committee to Win the Peace
Chicago Council of American-Soviet Friendship
Chicago Peace Society
Chinese Students Association[iii]
Christian Action Movement
Christian Brotherhood Movement
Christian Conference on War and Peace
Christian Front for Peace Against Fascism
Christian Pacifists in California
Christian Peace Conference
Church of England Peace League[iii]
Church Peace Union (also known as Council on Religious and International Affairs)
Churchmen's Committee for a Christian Peace
Citizens for Victory (formerly Committee to Defend America by Aiding the Allies)
Citizens Keep America Out of War Committee
Citizens Peace Petition Committee
Clearing House for Limitation of Armament
Collegiate Anti-Militarism League[iii]

Columbia University Youth Committee Against War
Comité Espagnol pour la Paix Civile[iii]
Commission on a Just and Durable Peace
Commission on Christian Education
Commission on Christian Social Action
Commission on International Justice and Goodwill
Commission on the Coordination of Efforts for Peace
Commission on World Peace of the Methodist Church
Commission to Study the Bases of a Just and Durable Peace
Commission to Study the Organization of Peace[iii]
Committee for a Democratic Far Eastern Policy
Committee for Legal Aid to Conscientious Objectors
Committee for National Morale
Committee for Nonviolent Action
Committee for Peace Day in the United Nations
Committee for Peaceful Alternatives
Committee on Drafting Youth
Committee on Education for International Goodwill. The Teachers' Union Auxiliary
Committee on Militarism in the Schools
Committee on Public Information
Committee to Defend America (see also, Citizens for Victory)
Committee to Defend America by Aiding the Allies (became Citizens for Victory, Jan. 1942)
Committee to Defend America by Keeping Out of War
Committee to Oppose Conscription of Women
Committee to Study the Basis of a Just and Durable Peace
Communist International
Community Relations Service
Concours Europeen de la Paix
Conference for Democracy and Terms of Peace
Conference of Clergymen of All Christian Churches
Conference on Cause and Cure of War
Conference on Christian Pacifists

Conference on Pacifist Philosophy of Life
Conference on Peace Research in History[iii]
Conference to Plan a Strategy for Peace
Congregational Education Society
Congrès Mondial Contre la Guerre imperialiste
Consultation on Christian Concern for Peace
Cultural and Scientific Conference for World Peace
D.A.R. Committee of Protest
Delaware Peace Society
Democratic Party National Committee
Deutsche Friedensgesellschaft[iii]
Deutscher Friedenskongress
Deutsches Friedenskomitee[iii]
Disarmament Education Committee
Disarmament Information Committee
Division of Peace and World Order, General Board of
  Christian Social Concerns of the Methodist Church
Duluth Peace Committee
Dunford House Cobden Memorial Association[i]
Economic and Disarmament Information Committee
Emergency Peace Campaign
Episcopal Pacific Fellowship
Equitist League
Federal Council of the Churches of Christ in America
Federation of International Polity Clubs
Fellowship of Reconciliation[i,iii]
Fellowship of Youth for Peace[iii]
Foreign Policy Association[iii]
Foundation for Promoting Enduring Peace
Free Religious Association of America
Friedensrat der Deutschen Demokratischen Republik
Friends Ambulance Unit
Friends Committee on National Legislation[i,iii]
Friends of Peace

Friends Service Committee
Friends World Conference Committee
Golden Rule Foundation
Great Lakes International Arbitration Society
Greater Philadelphia Committee Against Peacetime
    Conscription
Hague International Peace Conferences (1st, 2nd, and 3rd)
Henry Ford Peace Expedition
Henry Ford's Neutral Conference
Institut für Gesellschaftswissenschaften
Institute for Defense Analyses[iii]
Institute for Humane Studies
Institute for International Order
Institute of International Peace Studies
Interamerican Conference for the Maintenance of Peace
Intercollegiate Peace Association
Intergovernmental Conference for the Conclusion of an
    International Convention Concerning the Use of
    Broadcasting in the Cause of Peace
International Arbitration and Peace Association
International Arbitration League
International Conference of Women Workers to Promote
    Permanent Peace
International Conference on World Peace
International Convocation on the Requirements of Peace
International Institute for Peace[iii]
International Key Bureau
International Peace Academy Committee
International Peace Bureau[iii]
International Peace Campaign[iii]
International Peace Congress. The Hague
International Peace Forum[iii]
International Peace Research Association[iii]
International Peace Research Institute[iii]

International School of Peace
International Union
Internationales Institut für den Frieden
Inter-parliamentary Union[iii]
Japan Peace Society
June Calahan Foundation
Keep America Out of War Congress[iii]
Lafayette Institute
Latin American Institute
League for Permanent Peace
League for World Federation
League for World Peace
League of Nations[i,iii]
League of Nations Union
League of Peace and Freedom
League to Enforce Peace.[iii] American Branch
Library of the Peace Palace. The Hague, Netherlands
Liverpool Peace Society
Lobby for Peace
Maryland Peace Society[iii]
Massachusetts Peace Society
Mennonite Peace Problems Committee
Methodist Church
Ministers' No War Committee
National Catholic Welfare Conference
National Citizens' Commission on International Cooperation
National Civic Federation
National Civil Liberties Bureau
National Committee Against Peacetime Conscription Now
National Committee on Conscientious Objectors
National Committee on the Cause and Cure of War
National Congress of Peace and Friendship With the U.S.S.R.
National Council Against Conscription
National Council for Civil Liberties (Great Britain)

National Council for Conscientious Objectors
National Council for Reduction of Armaments
National Council for the Prevention of War[i,iii]
National Council to Abolish War
National Education Association of the United States. Research Division
National Emergency Committee
National Federation of Temple Sisterhoods[iii]
National Inter-Religious Conference on Peace
National Legation of the American People
National Peace Conference[iii]
National Peace Conference, Committe on Economics and Peace
National Peace Conversion Campaign
National Peace Council[i,iii]
National Peace Federation
National Peace Literature Service
National Security League[i,iii]
National Service Board for Religious Objectives
National Spiritual Assembly of the Baha'is of the U.S. and Canada
National Student Committee for the Limitation of Armament
National Student Forum on the Paris Pact
New England Arbitration and Peace Congress
New England Citizens Concerned for Peace
New Hampshire Peace Society
New History Foundation
New History Society
New York Peace Association
New York Peace Society[i,iii]
New York State War Council[iii]
New York Student Federation Against War
No Conscription Council
No More War Movement

Non-Violent Action Against Nuclear Weapons
Non-Violent Action Committee
Northern California Committee to Oppose Peacetime Conscription Now
Northern California Peace Society
Northern California Service Board for Conscientious Objectors
Ohio Peace Committee
Oklahoma Committee Against Compulsory Military Training
Organization of American Women for Strict Neutrality
Pacific Studies Center
Pacifica Associates
Palo Alto Peace Club[iii]
Paris Peace Conference of 1946
Patriotic Peace League
Peace Action Center
Peace Action Committee of Missouri
Peace Action Service
Peace and Disarmament Committee of the Women's International Organisations
Peace and Service Committee. Indiana Yearly Meeting of Friends
Peace Association of Friends in America.[iii] Richmond, Indiana
Peace Ballot Commission
Peace Builders
Peace Campaign
Peace Committee of Philadelphia
Peace Committee of the National Council of Women of the U.S. Voices of Peace
Peace Conference of the Asian and Pacific Regions
Peace Congress Committee
Peace Digest Associates[iii]
Peace Heroes Memorial Society
Peace House

Peace Information Center[iii]
Peace Now Movement
Peace Patriots[iii]
Peace Pilgrims
Peace Pledge Union[iii]
Peace Preparedness League[iii]
Peace Research Institute[iii]
Peace Research Society International
Peace Society of the City of New York
Peace Society, London[iii]
Peace Strategy Board
Peace Studies Institute[iii]
Peace Union of Finland
Peacemakers
Pennsylvania Arbitration and Peace Society
Pennsylvania Committee for Total Disarmament
Pennsylvania Peace Society
People for Peace
People's Congress for Democracy and Peace[iii]
People's Council of America[i,iii]
People's Council of America for Democracy and Peace
People's Freedom Union
People's Mandate Committee for Inter-American Peace and Cooperation
People's Mandate Committee to End War
People's Peace
Philadelphia Youth Council to Oppose Conscription
Physical Education Committee of Pennsylvania
Plea for Peace
Pledge for Peace Committee
Portland Women's Peace Council
Post War World Council
Promoting Enduring Peace
Rationalist Peace Society

Religious Society of Friends
Rotary International
Sacramento Peace Center[iii]
San Jose Peace Center[iii]
Schweizerische Friedensbewegung
Scientific Research Council on Peace and Disarmament
Socialist Party — Countries: Argentina; Bohemian Section; Canada; Committee for the Third International; Committee on Education and Research; German Section; Great Britain; India; Ireland; U.S
Société pour l'Arbitrage entre Nations[iii]
Society for the Prevention of WWIII
Society for the Promotion of Permanent and Universal Peace
Society of Friends (Great Britain)
South Dakota Peace Society
Soviet Peace Committee[iii]
Stockholm International Peace Research Institute
Strategy for Peace
Student Fellowship for Christian Life Service
Student Mobilization Committee to End the War in Vietnam
Student Peace Service[iii]
Student Peace Union
Tract Association of Friends
Union for Democratic Control
Unitarian Pacifist Fellowship
United Brotherhood Tolerance Movement
United Mothers World Peace Movement
United Pacifist Committee
United Peace Chest
United States Arms Control and Disarmament Agency[iii]
United World Federalists[iii]
Universal Peace Union[iii]
University of California. Associated Students. Peace Committee

University of New Brunswick. Centre for Conflict Studies[iii]
Vsesoiuznaia Konferentsiia Storonnikov Mira
War Resisters League[i,iii]
Wisconsin Peace Society
Woman's Christian Temperance Union
Woman's Peace Party[i,iii]
Woman's Republic
Women's Committee for World Disarmament
Women's Committee to Oppose Conscription
Women's National Committee to Keep U.S. out of War
Women's Peace Society[iii]
Women's Peace Union
World Alliance for International Friendship Through the Churches
World Assembly for Peace
World Citizens Association
World Committee Against War and Fascism
World Committee of Partisans of Peace
World Conference for International Peace Through Religion[iii]
World Conference of Representatives of National Peace Movements
World Congress Against War
World Council of Peace[iii]
World Liberalism
World Pacifist Meeting
World Peace Assembly
World Peace Association[iii]
World Peace Foundation[iii]
World Peace Stamp
World Peaceways[iii]
World Without War Council[i]
World Youth Peace
Y.M.C.A. Committee on Public Affairs of the National

Council of Y.M.C.A.s
Youth Committee Against War[iii]
Youth Movement for World Recovery

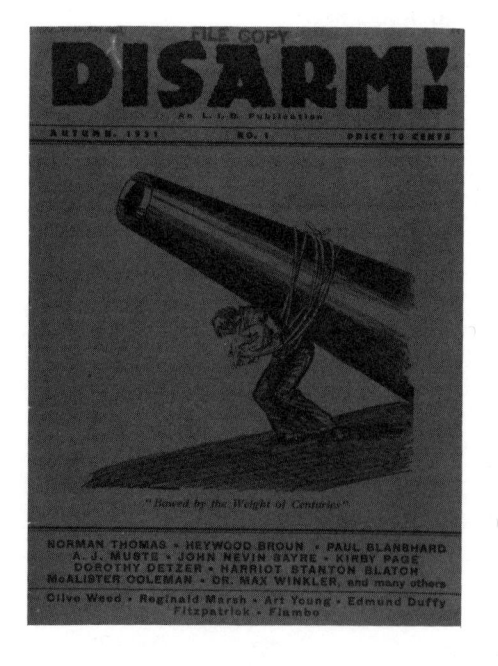

The burden of war is powerfully evoked on the cover of the first issue of *Disarm* (published by the League for Industrial Democracy).

The antiwar sentiments of American conscientious objectors during World War II are shown in this cover from *The Compass* (Civilian Public Service Camp publication).

PART III: SERIALS[9]

Absolutist War Objector Association. Brooklyn, New York, The Absolutist, 1943-1947

Across Frontiers. Berkeley. Spring 1984-

African Peace Research Institute, Nigeria. APRI Newsletter. 1988-

Agency, The. Washington, D.C. World Military Expenditures and Arms Transfers. 1966-1968, 1970-1972, 1985-1987

Almanach de la Paix par le Droit, Paris. 1905-1916.

American Academic Association for Peace in the Middle East, New York. Background Paper. 1981-1982

American Academic Association for Peace in the Middle East. Bulletin. 1972/73-

American Academic Association for Peace in the Middle East. Mideast Media Review. March 1989-

American Association for International Reconciliation. International Conciliation, 1907-1924. (Includes special bulletins. After 1924, published under the auspices of the Carnegie Endowment for International Peace. Division of Intercourse and Education)

American Friends Service Committee.[i,ii] Philadelphia, Pennsylvania. AFSC Quaker Service Bulletin. 1984-

American Friends Service Committee, Pasadena. Peace Service Bulletin. 1947-1954

American Friends Service Committee, Pasadena. Pacific Southwest Regional Office. Regional Bulletin. 1954, 1955

---

[9]Serials are defined as periodical publications that appear either in a numbered series or chronologically. These include bulletins, weeklies, monthlies, and annual reports.
 As a rule, titles are found under the name of the issuing agency. Thus, the Annual Report of the Carnegie Endowment for International Peace can be found under: Carnegie Endowment for International Peace. Annual Report.

American Friends Service Committee, Peace Education Committee. United States Anti-Apartheid Newsletter. Spring 1985 -

American Friends Service Committee. Peace Information Service, San Francisco. Peace News Wire. 1961

American League Against War and Fascism.[i,ii] American League Action Bulletin. Volume 1, number 1, 1935

American Movement for World Government. New York. World Peace News. 1971-1988

American Peace and Arbitration League.[ii] Bulletin. Numbers 18, 22, June 1915

American Peace Crusade.[ii] American Peace Crusader. Number 1, 1951

American Peace Mobilization.[ii] APM Newscaster. Number 1, 1941

American Peace Mobilization. APM Volunteer. Number 1, 1941

American Peace Mobilization. Bulletin. 1940-1941

American Peace Mobilization. News. 1941

American Peace Mobilization, New York City. Facts for Peace. 1941

American Peace Mobilization, Washington, D.C. Mobilize for Peace. 1940

American Peace Society.[i,ii] Advocate of Peace. 1894-1988

American Peace Society. Annual Report. 1884-1886, 1888, 1895, 1893, 1896, 1912-1924

American Peace Society, Washington. World Affairs. 1894-1988

American Peace Society of Japan. Bulletin. 1911-1912

American Purpose Washington, D.C. Jan. 1987-

American Society for Judicial Settlement[ii] of International Disputes, Baltimore. Judicial Settlement of International Disputes. Numbers 1-29. 1910-

American Union Against Militarism.[i,ii] Bulletin. 1916-1923

American University Union in Europe. Peace Series. 1920-1924

Amnesty Bulletin. New York, 1945-1948

Annuaire des Associations Internationales pour la Paix et la Société des Nations. 1924-1925

Annuaire du Mouvement Pacifiste. 1913

Arbeitsstelle Friedensforschung, Bonn. AFB-Info. 1986-

Arms Control. London, England. 1980-

Arms Control and Disarmament. Library of Congress, Washington, D.C. 1964-1973

Arms Control and Disarmament Agency,[ii] U.S. Documents on Disarmament. 1945

Arunachal Mission, Calcutta, India. World Peace. 1922-1945

Association de la Paix Par le Droit. Le Paix Par le Droit. 1890-1948

B.C.P.S. bulletin. Elgin, Illinois. 1946-1947 [publication for the men of Civilian Public Service]

Bertrand Russell Peace Foundation. Nottingham, England. The Spokesmen. 1970-1981/82

Bias. News-Peace. Integrity. Cooperation. 1954

Biosophical Review, New York. 1942-1944.

Books for Peace and Freedom (unbound). 1920

Buffalo Peace and Arbitration Society,[ii] Executive Committee. Report. 1911

Campaign for Nuclear Disarmament.[i,ii] London, England. Sanity. Voice of C.N.D. 1962-1983

Campaign for Peace and Democracy, East/West. Peace and Democracy News. Spring 1984-

Canada Peace Congress. Toronto. Peace News. 1973-1977

Canadian Disarmament Information Service,[ii] Toronto. The

Peace Calendar. 1983-

Canadian Disarmament Information Service, Toronto. Peace Magazine. March, 1985-

Canadian Institute for International Peace and Security,[ii] Ottawa. Annual Report. 1987/88, 1988/89

Canadian Institute for International Peace and Security, Ottawa. Background Paper. Oct. 1985-

Canadian Institute for International Peace and Security, Ottawa. A Guide to Canadian Policies on Arms Control, Disarmament, Defence and Conflict Resolution. 1985/86, 1987/88

Canadian Institute for International Peace and Security, Ottawa. Peace and Security. Spring 1986-Winter 1988/89

Canadian Institute for International Peace and Security, Ottawa. Peace in our time? 1989/1990-

Canadian Peace Congress.[ii] Toronto. Peace News. 1974-1977

Canadian Peace Research Institute,[ii] Oakville, Ontario. Peace Research. 1970

Canadian Peace Research Institute, Clarkson, Ontario. Peace Research Abstracts Journal. 1964-1989

Canadian Peace Research Institute. Peace Research Reviews. 1967-

Carnegie Endowment for International Peace.[i] Brief Reference List. Numbers 1-18. 1934-

Carnegie Endowment for International Peace. Division of Economics and History. Annual Report of the Director. 1922, 1924-1925

Carnegie Endowment for International Peace. Division of Intercourse and Education. Annual Report of the Director. 1916-1945

Carnegie Endowment for International Peace. Division of International Law, Washington, D.C. Monograph Series. Numbers 2, 4-6, 8. 1937-1945

Carnegie Endowment for International Peace. Library. Memoranda Series (unbound). 1940, 1942, 1947

Carnegie Endowment for International Peace, New York. Annual Report. 1948-1955

Carnegie Endowment for International Peace, Washington, D.C. Epitome of the Purpose, Plans and Methods of the Carnegie Endowment for International Peace. Abstract of the Year Book, 1919

Carnegie Endowment for International Peace, Washington, D.C. Year Book. 1911-29, 1931-33, 1936, 1939-1945, 1947

Catholic Association for International Peace,[ii] New York. C.A.I.P. News. 1939, 1942-1967

Center, The, Mountain View, California. Positive Alternatives. 1988

Center, The, New York, New York. Deadline 1990-

Center for Peace Studies, Akron. International Peace Studies Newsletter. 1976-1980, 1981-1983

Center for the Study of Democratic Institutions.[ii] Bulletin. 1961

Center for the Study of Democratic Institutions. Center Magazine. Oct./Nov. 1967-Nov./Dec. 1987

Center for the Study of Democratic Institutions. Center Report. Dec. 1971-Sept. 1976

Center for the Study of Democratic Institutions. Report of the President. 1959-1960

Center for War/Peace Studies,[ii] New York. Global Report. 1979-1987

Centre de Documentation et de Recherche Sur la Paix et les Conflits, Lyon. Damocles. April 1985-

Centre Interdisciplinaire[ii] de Recherches sur la Paix et d'Études Strategiques, Paris. Paix et Conflicts. 1983

Centro de Estudios de Movimientos Sociales, Madrid. A Priori. Numbers 3-13. 1982-1985

Centro de Informacion del Consejo Mundial de La Paz Para America y El Caribe. Cuban Movement for Peace and Sovereignty of the Peoples. 1980-

Challenge of Disarmament, New York. Mar. 31-July 10, 1932

Chinese Students Association,[ii] Manila. Democratic Youth: a Monthly Advocate for International Peace. Dec. 1938

Church of England Peace League,[ii] London. Annual Report, 1914-1918

Collegiate Anti-Militarism League, Lauionne PA. War? 1916-1918

Comité Espagnol pour la Paix Civile.[ii] Paris. La Paix Civile. December 1937-April 1939

Commission on Polish Affairs, Peace Conference 1919, Paris. Rapport. Numbers 2-5. 1919

Commission to Study the Organization of Peace,[ii] New York. Broadcasts, 1940.

Commission to Study the Organization of Peace. Report. Numbers 1-12, 20. 1940-

Committee on Education for Lasting Peace. Backlog for Action. Feb. 1944, Nov. 1948

Communist Information Bureau. For a Lasting Peace, for a People's Democracy. Rumania. 1947-1956

Communist Party. Great Britain. Peace Library. 1936

Conference for the Reduction and Limitation of Armaments, Geneva. Records of the Conference for the Reduction and Limitation of Armaments. Series A. Verbatim Records of Plenary Meetings. 1932

Conference on Peace Research in History and the Consortium on Peace Research, Education and Development.[ii] Rohnert Park, California. Peace and Change. 1972-1989

Conference on Science, Philosophy and Religion in their Relation to the Democratic Way of Life. Symposium. 1944, 1947-1948, 1953

Conference on the Discontinuance of Nuclear Weapons Tests,[i] Geneva. Verbatim Record of the 1st Plenary Meeting. Numbers 1-54, 56-273, 288, 292-295, 299-300. 1958-1961

Conferencia Interamericana Sobre Problemas de la Guerra y de la Paz, Mexico City. Diario. 1945

Conscription News, Washington D.C. 1944-1959.

Council on Religion and International Affairs, New York. Report. 1927, 1930, 1938-1942, 1945-53, 1956-1972

Current Military Literature. The Military Press, Oxford, England. 1983-1986

Current Thought on Peace and War. Hong Kong. 1960-1961, 1965-1968, 1972

De 3E Weg (i.e., De Derde Weg). May 1953-Sept. 1961

De Weg Naar Vrede. (related to De Derde Weg) Sept. 1952 - Dec. 1952/Jan. 1953

Defense de la Paix (Supesedes Les Partisans de la Paix). 1951-1954

Deutsche Gesellschaft für Friedens und Konfliktforschung. DGFK-Informationen. 1971-1983

Deutsche Gesellschaft für Friedens und Konfliktforschung. DGFK-Jahrbuch. 1979/80

Deutsche Friedensgesellschaft.[ii] Die Friedensbewegung. Berlin. 1925-1927

Deutscher Friedensrat, East Berlin. Information from the Peace Movement of the German Democratic Republic. 1953-1954, 1965-

Deutsches Friedenskomitee,[ii] Sekretariat, Berlin. Friedenswacht. 1952

Disarmament (Incorporated in Recovery, Geneva). 1931-1933

Disarmament and Arms Control. Oxford. 1963-1965

Dokumentation zur Abrustung und Sicherheit Bonn. Numbers 1-15. 1943-1959

Ecumenical Council of Churches in Czechoslovakia, Prague. Christian Peace Conference. 1963-1986

Fellowship of Reconciliation,[i,ii] London. Monthly News Sheet. 1924-

Fellowship of Reconciliation, New York. The Gist. 1944

Fellowship of Reconciliation, New York. News Sheet. 1917-1934, irregular

Fellowship of Reconciliation, New York. Peace Notes. 1948-1949

Fellowship of Reconciliation, Pacific Coast Office. Berkeley. California Newsletter. 1941-1951

Fellowship of Reconciliation, Pacific Coast Office. Berkeley. Northern California Reports. News Series. 1946-1949, irregular

Fellowship of Reconciliation, Pacific Coast Office. Berkeley. Northern California Reports. Quote Series, Aug. and Dec. 1946, Jan. 1947

Fellowship of Reconciliation, Pacific Coast Office. Berkeley. Northern California Reports. Research Series, Feb. 1949

Fellowship of Reconciliation, Pacific Coast Office. Pasadena, California. Peacemaker. June 1940

Fellowship of Reconciliation, Toronto. Reconciliation. 1944-1947

Fellowship of Youth for Peace,[ii] New York. Bulletin, 1925

Fight for Peace and Democracy (sometimes published as Fight Against War and Fascism). 1933-1939

Foreign Economic Administration, Technical Industrial Disarmament Committee, Washington, D.C. T.I.D.C. Project. Numbers 5, 8, 11-12, 15, 18-19, 26, 30-31. 1945

Foreign Policy Association,[ii] New York. Foreign Policy Committee Reports. Nov. 1933-Mar. 1934

Forschungsinstitut für Friedenspolitik, West Germany. Friedens Brief. Jan./Feb. 1989

Foundation for P.E.A.C.E. Peace in Action. 1986-

Die Frau in Unserer Zeit (Konrad-Adenauer-Stiftung). Jan. 1983-

Fredsposten. Helsingfors, Finland. 1982-1988

Der Friedens Kampfer. Berlin. 1929-1933

Die Friedens-Warte. Berlin. 1899-1986

Friedensblätter des Verbandes Deutscher Handlunggehilfen zu

Leipzig. Leipzig, Germany. Numbers 1, 3-6, n.d.

Der Friedensbote. Ein Sonntagsblatt für Stadt und Land. Hamburg, Germany. July 16-23, 1916 and Oct. 1949

Friedensglocke. Bremen, Germany. 1914

Der Friedensruf. Schaffhausen, Switzerland. 1917-1918

Der Friedensvertrag. Berlin, Germany. 1921-1922

Friedenszeitung. Zurich, Switzerland. 1982-1986

Friends Committee on National Legislation.[i,ii] Annual Report. 1953

Friends Committee on National Legislation. FCNL Action. 1960

Friends Committee on National Legislation. Washington Newsletter. Nov. 1943-Aug. 1962

Friends' Peace Service Letter. Philadelphia. 1945, 1947

Friends of Kenya. Friends of Kenya. May 1987-

Gaceta de Paz. Argentina. (Revista de Jurisprudencia. Boletín informativo diario de todos los fueros) 1962, 1967

Great Britain. War Office. Daily Review of the Foreign Press. 1915-1919

Herald of Peace, Lemoore, CA. 1927-1928

Herald of Peace and International Arbitrations. London. (London, Peace Society). 1903-1920

Hessische Stiftung Friedens und Konfliktforschung, Frankfurt am Main. Friedensgutachten. 1987-

Hollywood Peace Forum. Los Angeles. Publications. 1940-

The Idealist: for Democracy, Peace, Race Tolerance. New York. 1938, 1941, 1948

Independent Labour Party, London. Women's Peace Crusade Leaflets. Numbers 6-8. n.d.

Independent Labour Party, Manchester and London. Road to Peace Leaflets. Numbers 1-6. n.d.

Institut Français de Polemologie, Paris. Etudes Polemologiques. (Supersedes Guerres et Paix) 1971-1988

Institut Français de Polemologie, Paris. Guerres et Paix: Revue Trimestrielle. 1967-1970

Institut für Friedensforschung. Vienna. Wiener Blätter Zur Friedensforschung. 1974-1985

Institute, The, Ottawa. Points of View. Mar. 1986-

Institute for Defense Analyses,[ii] Washington D.C./Los Angeles. Annual Report. 1961, 1965-1966, 1968-1969

Institute for Defense Analyses, Washington, D.C. Research Paper. Numbers 2-3, 6, 24-79, 140-774. 1963-

Institute for the Study of Nonviolence. Palo Alto, California. Journal. 1966-1969, 1972-1974

Institutt for Fredsforskning, Norway. Journal of Peace Research. 1964-

International Conference for Disarmament and Peace, London. Peace Press (supersedes Peace Information Bulletin). 1965-1981

International Dialogue Commentaries and Studies. London. June 1983-July 1984

International Freedom Foundation, Washington D.C. Angola Peace Monitor. 1989-

International Institute for Peace,[ii] Vienna. Current Articles, Interviews, and Statements on Disarmament, Peaceful Coexistence, and International Cooperation. 1961-.

International Institute for Peace, Vienna. Documents and Papers on International Problems Relative to World Peace. Numbers 38-53. 1960-1963

International Labour Office. Geneva. Official Bulletin. 1919-1923

International Peace Bureau,[ii] Berne. Correspondence Bi-Mensuelle. 1895-1911

International Peace Bureau, Berne. Die Friedensbewegung; organ des Internationalen Friedensbureau. 1912-1913

International Peace Bureau, Berne. Peace Information

Bulletin. 1963

International Peace Bureau, Berne. The Peace Movement. 1912-1914

International Peace Bureau, Berne. Procès-Verbal des Seances de la Commission du Bureau. 1912, 1914

International Peace Bureau, Berne. Rapport de Gestion pour l'Annee... 1922-1926

International Peace Bureau, Geneva. Geneva Monitor Disarmament. 1989-

International Peace Campaign, Stockholm. Meddelande. 1944

International Peace Campaign. News Letter. 1938-1939

International Peace Campaign. Swedish Committee. Verksamhetsberuttelse. 1944

International Peace Campaign. Durban, South Africa. Peace. Oct. and Nov. 1938

International Peace Congress. Publications. 1915

International Peace Forum. Peace. Mar.-Sept. 1912

International Peace Forum. New York. Peace Forum. 1914-1915 (1912-1915 on microfiche)

International Peace Forum, New York. World Court. 1915-1919

International Peace Research Association, Brussels, Belgium. Science et Paix. Revue Internationale de Recherches sur la Paix, le Conflit, et le Developpement. 1973, numbers 1-194

International Peace Research Association, Lancaster, England. International Peace Research Newsletter. 1972; 1989-

International Peace Research Association, Oslo. International Peace Research Newsletter. 1972-1987

International Peace Research Association, Rio de Janeiro. International Peace Research Association Newsletter. Aug. 1987-Jan. 1989

International Peace Research Institute, Oslo. Bulletin of Peace Proposals. 1970-1987

Inter-parliamentary Union.[ii] Annuaire de l'Union Interparlementaire. 1911-1914

Inter-parliamentary Union. Scandinavian Group. Aarbog for de Nordiske Interparlamentariske Grupper. 1918-1925

Inter-parliamentary Union, Scandinavian Group. Meddelelser Fra de Nordiske Interparlamentariske Grupper. 1918-21

Israel at Peace. Tel Aviv. 1972 (see below under Miflaga Komunistit Yisraelit. MAKI)

Jahrbuch für Volkerrecht und Friedensbewegung .. Leipzig. Numbers 1-2

Jewish-Arab Association for Peace and Equality. Bulletin. 1956

Journal of Conflict Resolution, Ann Arbor. (Supersedes Research Exchange on the Prevention of War Bulletin). 1957-1989

Keep America Out of War Congress.[ii] War, What For.1938

Klub der Deutschen Sozialdemokratischen Abgeordneten, Vienna. Die Taetigkeit der Deutschen Sozialdemokratischen Abgeordneten im Oesterreichischen Reichsrat. Numbers 1-4, 9-10. 1912-1919

Konrad-Adenauer-Stiftung. Die Frau in Unserer Zeit. Jan. 1983-

League for Industrial Democracy. New York. Disarm! 1931

League for World Peace. Journal. Volume 1, Number 1. 1940?

League of Nations.[i,ii] International Trade Statistics. 1931-1938

League of Nations. Journal Officiel. 1920-1940

League of Nations. Memorandum on International Trade and Balance of Payments. 1927-1931

League of Nations. Memorandum on Public Finance. 1922-1926

League of Nations. Money and Banking. 1936-1945

League of Nations. Monthly Summary of the League of Nations. Apr. 1921-Feb. 1940

League of Nations. Report on the Work of the League. 1920-1943/44

League of Nations. Statistical Yearbook of the Trade in Arms, Ammunitions, and Implements of War. 1924, 1926-1938

League of Nations. Work of the Health Organization. 1923, 1927-1931

League of Nations. Yearbook of the League of Nations. 1921/22-1926, 1927/28

League to Enforce Peace,[ii] New York. The League Bulletin. 1917-1919

Life and Peace Institute, Uppsala. Life and Peace Review. 1987-

Maryland Peace Society,[ii] Baltimore. Maryland Quarterly. 1910-1912

Medical Association for Prevention of War. London. Journal. 1981-1984

Medical Association for Prevention of War. London. Proceedings. 1968-1981

Medical Peace Campaign, London. Bulletin. 1938

Messenger for Peace, The. 1913-1927

Mid-Peninsula Peace Center, Palo Alto, CA. Peaceworks. 1989-

Miflaga Komunistit Yisraelit (MAKI). Tel Aviv. Information Bulletin. 1967-1972 (title changed to Israel at Peace in 1972.)

Mir. (Published by Ceskoslovensky vybor obrancu miru). Prague. 1968-1970

Mir: Zhurnal na Rasskom Iazyke Izdaetsia Sovetskim Komitetom Zashchitz Mira, Moscow. 1950-51

Mir Chez Suiuziavane, Numbers 1-2, 1919

Mir Ctvrtletnik Pro Obranu Miru, Czechoslovakia. 1949

Mir i Razoruzhenie. Moscow. 1980, 1982, 1984, 1986-1987

Mount Holyoke Institute on the United Nations, South Hadley, MA. Selected Speeches. 1949

Movimiento Cubano por la Paz y la Soberanía de los Pueblos,

La Habana. Sintesis Informativa. 1987-

National Council for the Prevention of War,[i,ii] Seattle Branch, Seattle, Washington. Peacemaker. April 1941

National Council for the Prevention of War, Washington, D.C. International Notes for Disarmament and World Recovery. 1933-1934

National Council for the Prevention of War, Washington, D.C. News Bulletin. 1921-1934

National Council for the Prevention of War, Washington, D.C. Peace Action. 1934-1968

National Council for the Prevention of War, Washington, D.C. Peace Voter News. June and October, 1938

National Council for the Prevention of War, Washington, D.C. Washington Information Letter. 1937-1939, 1940, 1941, irregular

National Council for the Prevention of War, Western Office, San Francisco. News Bulletin. Oct. 1921-May 1934

National Council for the Prevention of War, Western Office, San Francisco. Report. 3rd Series, 1935

National Council for the Prevention of War, Western Office, San Francisco. Report Letter. Aug. 1936 - Mar. 1937

National Council for the Prevention of War, Western Office, San Francisco. Report on Naval Conference. 1935-1936

National Council of Returned Peace Corps Volunteers, Washington, D.C. Worldview Magazine. Summer 1981-

National Federation of Temple Sisterhoods.[ii] Peace News Flashes. 1940-1941

National Peace Conference,[ii] New York. Annual Report. 1939/40

National Peace Conference, New York. Bulletin. 1938-1951

National Peace Conference, New York. Geneva Information Service. 1939

National Peace Conference, New York. Inter-council News Letter. 1938-1939

National Peace Conference, New York. Washington Information Service. 1937/38-1941

National Peace Conference (in cooperation with Foreign Policy Association Incorporated). World Affairs Pamphlets. Numbers 1-9

National Peace Council,[i,ii] London. Economic Series. 1911

National Peace Council, London. Educational Series. 1908-1913

National Peace Council, London. General Series. 1913-1915

National Peace Council, London. International Declarations. Number 1, 1945

National Peace Council, London. Monthly Circular. 1913, 1914-1920

National Peace Council, London. NPC Papers. 1946-1947

National Peace Council, London. One World. (Supersedes Peace Aims). 1946-1958

National Peace Council, London. Peace, a Monthly Review of the Peace Movement. April 1933-October 1941

National Peace Council, London. Peace Aims Documents. Numbers 1-4. 1942-

National Peace Council, London. Peace Aims Pamphlets. Numbers 1-60. 1940-

National Peace Council, London. Peace Year Book. 1920-1922, 1927, 1932-1942, 1944-1955

National Peace Council, London. Political Series. 1908-1912

National Peace Council, London. Report. 1914-20, 1944-1966 (To 1944 titled Annual Report)

National Peace Council, London. Social Reform Series. 1912

National Peace Council, London. Towards World Government. Numbers 1-2. 1948-1950

National Peace Council, London. Information Office, London. American Opinion. 1947-1948

National Peace Council, London. Information Office, London.

Reading and Reference Notes. 1947, 1948

National Peace Council of New Zealand. Monthly Circular. 1914

National Security League.[i,ii] Bulletin. 1942

National Security League. General Letter. Dec. 1942 - Aug. 1946

National Security League. Patriotism Through Education Series. 1917-1918

National Security League. Report. 1940-1941, 1944

National Security League. Research Bulletin. Sept. 1944

Neutral Conference for Continuous Mediation,[i] Stockholm. Neutral Conference Documents. 1916-

New York Peace Information Service, New York. The Poor Man's Guide to War/Peace Literature. 1964

New York Peace Information Center, New York. Where in the World? 1964

New York Peace Society,[i,ii] New York. Messenger of the New York Peace Society. Nov. 1917-May 1920

New York Peace Society, New York. News Letter. 1929-1939

New York Peace Society. Yearbook. 1907-1919

New York State War Council.[ii] War Digest. 1941-1942

Novosti Press Agency, Moscow. Disarmament and Security. 1961-1962

Nuclear Disarmament. Oslo. 1982, 1983 (numbers 6, 7)

Nuclear Times. New York. 1982-

Obiezione. Bellinzona, Lugano. 1970-1973

Obshchestvo Mira v Moskvie. 1909-1910

Oesterreichische Friedensgesellschaft. Vienna. Der Friedensfreund. 1914

L'Organisation Politique et Economique du Monde. Paris. La Paix des Peuples; Revue Internationale de l'Organisation

Politique et Economique du Monde.
February 25 - April 10, 1919 and June 25, 1919

Pace e Libertà. Milan. 1954

Pacifica Center Associates of Los Angeles. Peace Digest. 1945

Pacifist Research Bureau.[i] Quarterly Research Survey.
1947-1949

Pacifistisch Socialistische Partij. Bevrijding.
Feb. 1958-Dec. 1966

La Paix: Journal Libre Renseignant sur les Faits Generaux de la Guerre et le Mouvement des Idées au Front. Belgium. 1918

La Paix. Journal Politique, d'Economie Social et Financiere.
Berlin. Feb. 1917-Nov. 1918

La Paix Mondiale: Journal pour la Reconciliation des Peuples. Berlin. Dec. 19, 1918

La Paix Organisée. Neuilly-sur-Seine. 1917-1920

La Paix: Revue Internationale de Critique Pacifiste.
Paris. April, July 1934

Palo Alto Peace[ii] Club. Flashlight, Palo Alto. 1953-1962

Paris Peace Conference, 1919.[i] La Paix de Versailles. 1929-1939

Paris Peace Conference, 1919. Preliminary Peace Conference Protocol. Jan. 18-May 31, 1919

Paris Peace Conference, 1919. Recueil des Actes de la Conference. 1922-1934

Peace Action Coalition. Cleveland, Ohio. 1970

Peace and Freedom News. Berkeley.
Mar. 4 and Aug. 29, 1968

Peace and Goodwill, a sequel to the Olive Leaf.
Wisbech, England. 1912, 1914, 1916-1921, 1931

Peace Association of Friends in America.[ii] Richmond, Indiana.
The Messenger of Peace. 1913-1927.

Peace Balloon. (See also Underground Newspaper Microfilm Collection PN4827.U55).

Peace Digest Associates. Peace Digest. 1933-1946

Peace Information Center.[ii] Peacegram. 1950

Peace News. New York. 1943-1946.

Peace News. St. Petersburg, Florida. 1944-1945

Peace News for Nonviolent Revolution (microfilm). 1973-1978

Peace News, Ltd., London. Peace News: the International Pacifist Weekly. 1950-1974

Peace Newsletter. (See also Underground Newspaper Microfilm Collection PN4827.U55). 1973-1975, 1983

Peace Now. New York, 1990-

The Peace of Tomorrow. Detroit, Michigan. September 1940

Peace Patriots.[ii] Arbitrator. 1918-1943

Peace Plans. Berrima, Australia. Numbers 1-12, 14-26

Peace Plans (Libertarian Microfiche Publications). Numbers 27/28

Peace Pledge Union, London. Bond of Peace. 1940

Peace Pledge Union, London. Peace News (microfilm). 1968-1969

Peace Preparedness League. Preparedness. 1916

Peace Progress. National Cash Register Co. Dec. 1925

Peace Research Institute.[ii] Dundas, Ontario. Peace Research Abstracts. 1988-

Peace Research Institute. Oslo. Journal of Peace Research. 1964-1989

Peace Research Institute. Frankfurt. Prif Reports Frankfurt. Number 1, Winter 1987-

Peace Society, London.[ii] Pamphlets on War and Peace. Numbers 1-96

Peace Societies of the District of Columbia. The Crisis. Jan. 25, 1916

Peace Studies Institute.[ii] Bulletin. 1977-

Peacebuilder, Takoma Park, Maryland, 1990-

Peacemaker Movement. Peacemaker. 1949-

People's Congress for Democracy and Peace.[ii] The Congress Builder. 1937

People's Council of America,[i,ii] New York. Bulletin. 1917-1919

Pokoj i Wolnosc. Paix et Liberte. Biuletyn Sekcji Polskiej organizacji "Pokoj i Wolnosc." 1951-1956

Post War Bureau, London. War and Peace Aims Digest. 1940

Prison Views. Philadelphia, Pennsylvania, 1947-1949 [news of conscientious objectors]

Problemas de la Paz y del Socialismo (Revista Teórica e Informativa de la Actualidad Internacional). 1965, 1967-1968, 1971-1972

Professors World Peace Academy, New York, New York. PWPA International Special Report. 1983, 1986-1987

Research Institute for Peace and Security. Asian Security. 1979-1984, 1987-1988

Respect for Life. Linz, Austria. World Peace Press. 1980-

Revue des Balkans: Politique, Diplomatique, Finances... Paris. 1919

Rijksuniversiteit te Groningen. Polemologisch Instituut. Assen, Netherlands. Nieuwe Literatuur Over Oorlog en Vrede. 1964-1967

Ruestung und Abruestung, Berlin. 1874-1888, 1931-1935

Sacramento Peace Center.[ii] Sacramento, California. Peace Currents. 1966-1969

San Jose Peace Center.[ii] San Jose, California. Peace Times. 1966-1968, 1973-1977, 1979

Sanity. Peace-Oriented News and Comment. Montreal, Canada. 1966-1967

Sicherheit und Friedliche Zusammenarbeit in Europa. Berlin. 1954-1967, 1975-1981

Sipri Yearbook of World Armaments and Disarmament. Stockholm. 1968/69-1969/70, 1972-

Società Internationale Per la Pace. Pro Pace. 1896-1920, 1929-1937

Société de la Paix de Moscow. Obshchestvo mira v Moskvie. 1909-1910

Société pour l'Arbitrage Entre Nations.[ii] Paris. Revue de la Paix. 1903-1911; 1923

Society for Social Responsibility in Science. Gambier, Ohio. S.S.R.S. Newsletter. 1951-1952, 1954, 1964-1966

Soviet Peace Committee,[ii] Moscow. The Twentieth Century and Peace. 1970-1988

Stanley Foundation, Muscatine, Iowa. Conference to Plan a Strategy for Peace. Report. 1966

Stanley Foundation, U.S. Foreign Policy Conference. Strategy for Peace. 1987

Statements on War and Peace Aims. 1939-1944

Stockholm International Peace Research Institute. The Arms Race and Arms Control. 1982-1984

Student Peace Service.[ii] Los Angeles, California. Peace Points. January, April 1939

Sudan. Southern Region. Ministry of Information, Culture, Youth, and Sports. Peace and Progress. 1972/73-

Swarthmore College Library, Swarthmore, PA. Peace Collection. Peace Collection Bulletin. Numbers 1-12. 1947-

Tampere Peace Research Institute, Finland. Instant Research on Peace and Violence. 1971-1977

Tampere Peace Research Institute, Finland. Current Research on Peace and Violence. 1978-

Tapri Yearbook. Aldershot, Avebury. 1986-

Ulster Association for Peace with Honour, Belfast. The Ulster Bulletin. 1922-1925

Unidad de Información, San José, Costa Rica. Programa de Apoyo a la Paz, la Cooperación y el Desarrollo en

Centroamérica. Documentos. 1988-

Union of Concerned Scientists. Catalyst. 1986-

United Italy Society of Great Britain, London. Problems of the Peace Congress. Number 1

United Nations. Centre Against Apartheid. (in cooperation with the World Peace Council.) International Mobilisation. June-November 1983, Apr. 12, 1974

United Nations. Centre for Disarmament, New York. Disarmament Yearbook. 1977, 1979-1988

United Nations.[i] Conference of the Committee on Disarmament, Geneva. Basic Information for Delegations on Conference Arrangements and Documents. Numbers 7-11, 17, 18-21, 23. 1966-1973

United Nations. Conference of the Committee on Disarmament, Geneva. Checklist of Documents. Numbers 35,37-41, 44, 47-48. 1965-1970

United Nations. Conference of the Committee on Disarmament, Geneva. Final Verbatim Record. Numbers 1-29. Mar. 1962-Aug. 1974

United Nations. Conference of the Committee on Disarmament, Geneva. List of Members of Delegations to the Conference. Numbers 22-39, 40-41, 43-44, 46-48, 50-52, 54-55. 1965-1974

United Nations. Department for Disarmament Affairs, New York. Disarmament Newsletter. 1983-

United Nations. Educational, Scientific and Cultural Organization. UNESCO Yearbook On Peace and Conflict Studies. 1980-

United Nations General Assembly and Disarmament. New York. 1985-1986

United Nations. General Assembly. Committee on Disarmament at U.N. Headquarters. Disarmament Times. 1980-

U.S. Arms Control and Disarmament Agency.[ii] Washington, D.C. Arms Control Report. 1962, 1965, 1968-1973, 1976-

U.S. Arms Control and Disarmament Agency. Documents on Disarmament. 1945

109

U.S. Arms Control and Disarmament Agency. Publication. Numbers 1-78, 1961-

U.S. Arms Control and Disarmament Agency. World Military Expenditures and Arms Trade. 1963

U.S. Arms Control and Disarmament Agency. World Military Expenditures and Related Data. 1965-1966, 1969

U.S. Congress. Senate. Committee on Foreign Relations. Neutrality, Peace Legislation, and Our Foreign Policy. . 1939

U.S. Department of State,[i] Washington, D.C. Disarmament Document Series. 1961-1962

U.S. Department of State, Washington, D.C. Disarmament Series. Numbers 1-5. 1961-

United States Institute of Peace, Washington, D.C. The United States Institute of Peace Journal. 1990-

United World Federalists,[ii] Student Division. Scarsdale, New York. The Student Federalist. 1943, 1945-1949

Universal Peace Union.[ii] Philadelphia, Pennsylvania. The Peacemaker and Court of Arbitration. 1894

Universitets Forlaget, Oslo, Norway. Bulletin of Peace Proposals. 1970-1979

Universities Committee on Post-War International Problems, Boston. Problems. 1943-1945

University of New Brunswick. Centre for Conflict Studies.[ii] Conflict Quarterly. 1980-

University of Sussex, Brighton, Sussex, England. Armament and Disarmament Information Unit. ADIU Report. 1985-

Utsunomiya Gunshuku Kenkyushitsu, Tokyo. Gunshuku Fmondai Shiry O. 1980-

V Zashchiut Mira, Moscow. 1951-1961

Verlag Wissenschaft und Politik, Koln FRG. Koelner Ringvorlesung zu Fragen von Frieden und Krieg. 1984-1985

Via Pacis. Orbis Press Agency, Prague. 1987-

Vsemirnyi Kongress Storonnikov Mira. Postoiannyi Komitet,

Moscow. Mir. 1950-1951

War/Peace Report, New York. 1961-1975

War Resisters League,[i,ii] New York. The Nonviolent Activist. December 1984 and Volumes 2-3, 1985-

War Resisters League, New York. W.R.L. News. 1945-1964, 1967-1968, 1971-

War Resisters League, New York. WIN. Peace and Freedom Through Non-Violent Action. 1967-1974

Wisbech Local Peace Association, Wisbech. Reports. 1917-1920.

Witness for Peace [United Kingdom] in association with Church Action for Central America (CAFCA). Richmond, Surrey. What We Have Seen and Heard in Nicaragua. 1986-1987

Women's International Democratic Federation, Berlin. Information Bulletin. 1946

Women's International Democratic Federation, Berlin. Unity for the Defence of Our Rights, of Our Children, of Peace. 1953-1954

Women's International League for Peace and Freedom, Boston. News of the United States Section. 1926, 1930-1932

Women's International League for Peace and Freedom. British Section. Monthly News Sheet. 1916-1919, 1924, 1934-1935

Women's International League for Peace and Freedom. British Section. Yearly Reports. 1918, 1923

Women's International League for Peace and Freedom, Chicago. Yearbook. 1916

Women's International League for Peace and Freedom. Danish Section. Fred Og Frihed. 1926, 1934, 1941

Women's International League for Peace and Freedom, Geneva. Bulletin. 1920-1924

Women's International League for Peace and Freedom.[i] Geneva. Circular Letters. 1936-1940

Women's International League for Peace and Freedom, Geneva. International Congress of the Women's

International League for Peace and Freedom. 1915-1932, 1937-1971

Women's International League for Peace and Freedom, Geneva. International News. 1947-1948

Women's International League for Peace and Freedom, Geneva. News Letter from Geneva. 1924-1925

Women's International League for Peace and Freedom, Geneva. Pax et Libertas. 1920, 1925-1940, 1949-1957, 1960

Women's International League for Peace and Freedom, Geneva. Pax Special. 1925

Women's International League for Peace and Freedom. German Section. Völkerversöhnende Frauenarbeit. 1914-1931

Women's International League for Peace and Freedom, New York. International Circular Letter. 1941-1948

Women's International League for Peace and Freedom, New York. News Sheet. 1941-1948

Women's International League for Peace and Freedom, 9th Congress, La Lacovice, 1937. Circular Letter on Congress. 1937

Women's International League for Peace and Freedom. Norwegian Section. Fred og Frihet. 1950-1951

Women's International League for Peace and Freedom. Swedish Section. Arsberattelse. 1923-1925, 1939-1944

Women's International League for Peace and Freedom. Swedish Section. Fred och Frihet. 1939-1940, 1942-1945

Women's International League for Peace and Freedom. United States Section. Annual Report. 1923/24

Women's International League for Peace and Freedom. United States Section. Bulletin. 1920-1922, 1923-1925

Women's International League for Peace and Freedom. United States Section. California State Branch, Saratoga. Bulletin. 1962

Women's International League for Peace and Freedom. United States Section. Labor Letter. 1937

Women's International League for Peace and Freedom. United States Section. Los Angeles Branch. Peace Brevities. 1936-1938

Women's International League for Peace and Freedom. United States Section. Peace and Freedom. 1981-1982

Women's International League for Peace and Freedom. Washington, D.C. Four Lights. 1917-1953, 1963-1966

Women's International League for Peace and Freedom. Washington, D.C. Washington Newsletter. 1949, 1957, 1967

Women's International Organization. Peace and Disarmament Committee. Annual Report. 1932, 1936/37-1940

Women's International Organization. Peace and Disarmament Committee, Geneva. Press Release. 1932, 1936-1940

Women's Peace Society.[ii] News Letter. 1926-1930

The Word in the Service of an Understanding Between All Mankind. The Hague (also in microfilm). Aug. 12, 1919-Oct. 18, 1919

World Citizens Assembly, San Francisco, CA. World Citizen. 1982-1983, 1985

World Conference for International Peace[ii] Through Religion, New York. Publication. 1928-37

World Conference on World Peace through the Rule of Law. World Peace Through Law. 1963-

World Council of Peace,[ii] Helsinki. Documents. 1970, 1971

World Council of Peace, Helsinki. Information Bulletin. 1966-1967

World Council of Peace, Helsinki. Perspectives. 1967-1969

World Council of Peace, Vienna. Bulletin. 1959-1966, 1968

World Federalist Association. World Federalist. 1982-1984

World Festival of Youth and Students for Peace and Friendship, Moscow. Information Bulletin. 1957-1958

World Order, New York. (Supersedes World Unity). 1935-1949

World Peace Association.[ii] World Government Advocate.

World Peace Congress, Paris. Los Partidarios de la Paz/Les Partisans de la Paix. 1949

World Peace Congress, Paris. World Peace Congress Bulletin/Prague Section. World Peace Congress Bulletin. 1949

World Peace Council,[i] Helsinki. Peace Courier. (Supersedes Perspectives). 1970-1988

World Peace Council. Information Centre. Programme of Action. 1979, 1983

World Peace Foundation,[ii] Boston. America Looks Ahead, Numbers 1-12. 1941-1946

World Peace Foundation, Boston. Annual Report. 1912-1918

World Peace Foundation, Boston. Documents on American Foreign Relations. 1938/39-1970

World Peace Foundation, Boston. Studies in Citizen Participation in International Relations. Numbers 1-2, 4-6. 1959-1960

World Peace Foundation. World Affairs Books. Numbers 1-20. 1933-1935

World Peace Library Association. The Mace Bulletin. Numbers 1, 3, 1944

World Peace Newsletter, Chicago. 1940, 1942, 1946

World Peace Report, 1990-

World Peaceways.[ii] Bulletin. 1936

World Peaceways. Information Service. 1937-1940

World Peaceways. The Neutral World. Number 1, 1940

World Peaceways. Peaceways Forum. 1937-1940

World Peaceways. World Observer. 1937-1940

World Unity; a Monthly Magazine Interpreting the Spirit of the New Age. (Superseded by World Order) 1927-1935

World Veterans Federation. International Information Center

on Peace-keeping Operations, Paris. Documentation. Numbers 1-4

World Veterans Foundation, Paris. Disarmament. 1964-1967

Youth Committee Against War.[ii] Anti-War News Service. 1940-1941.

Za Mir i Bezopasnost Naradov, Moscow. 1966-1970, 1971, 1985-1986

Za Mir i Trud (Russian news collection, Novocherkassk). 1895, 1898-1905, 1906

Zionism, Enemy of Peace and Social Progress. Progress, Moscow. 1985-1988

BIBLIOGRAPHY

Adams, Ephraim Douglass. The Hoover War Collection at Stanford University, California. A Report and an Analysis. Stanford: Stanford University Press, 1921.

Almond, Nina, and Lutz, Ralph Haswell. An Introduction to the Bibliography of the Paris Peace Conference. Stanford: Stanford University Press, 1935.

Almond, Nina and Fisher, H.H. Special Collections in the Hoover Library on War, Revolution, and Peace. Stanford: Stanford University Press, 1940.

Biographical Dictionary of Modern Peace Leaders. Edited by Harold Josephson. Westport, Connecticut: Greenwood Press, 1985.

Card Catalog of the Library of the Peace Palace at the Hague, 1913-1970. Edited by Warren F. Kuehl. Clearwater Publishing Company, Inc., 1980.

A Catalog of Paris Peace Conference Delegation Propaganda in the Hoover War Library. Stanford: Stanford University Press, 1926.

Dedication of the Hoover Library on War, Revolution, and Peace. Stanford: Stanford University Press, 1941.

Fine, Melinda, and Steven, Peter M. American Peace Directory. Cambridge, Massachusetts: Institute for Peace and Disarmament Studies, 1984.

Glazier, Kenneth Maclean, and Hobson, James R. International and English-Language Collections: A Survey of Holdings at the Hoover Institution on War, Revolution, and Peace. Stanford: Hoover Institution Press, 1971.

Guide to Swarthmore College Peace Collection, 2nd edition, Swarthmore, Pennsylvania, 1981.

Hoover Institution on War, Revolution and Peace. Stanford: Stanford University Press, 1963.

"The Hoover War Library," in Concerning Stanford. Vol. 1, no. 9, June 1925.

International Peace Directory. Edited by T. Woodhouse. Plymouth, England: Northcote House Publishers, 1988.

The Library of the Hoover Institution. Edited by Peter Duignan. Stanford: Hoover Institution Press, 1985.

McLean, Philip T. Archival, Manuscript, and Special Collections in the General Library of the Hoover Institution. Vol. 1, 1968.

McLean, Philip T. "The Hoover Institute and Library." The Library Quarterly, vol. XIX, no. 4, October 1949.

Meyer, Robert S. Peace Organizations Past and Present. Jefferson, North Carolina: McFarland & Company, 1988.

Palm, Charles G. and Reed, Dale. Guide to the Hoover Institution Archives. Stanford: Hoover Institution Press, 1980.

Peace Archives: A Guide to Library Collections of the Papers of American Peace Organizations and of Leaders in the Public Effort for Peace. Edited by Marguerite Green. Berkeley: The World Without War Council, 1986.

Peace Movements of the World. Edited by Alan J. Day. Harlow, Essex: Longman Press, 1986.

Peace Research in Western Europe: A Directory Guide. Edited by Robert Rudney. Washington D.C., 1989.

Wittner, Lawrence S. Rebels Against War. Philadelphia: Temple University Press, 1984.

World Directory of Peace Research and Training Institutions. 6th ed. Prepared by the Sector of Social and Human Services, New York: Unesco, 1988.

World Encyclopedia of Peace, volumes 1-4. Edited by Linus Pauling. Oxford: Pergamon Press, 1986.

Guide to John D. Crummey Peace Collection

INDEX

Abrams, Irwin	15
Across Frontiers	89
Adair, Fred Lyman	15
Adams, Ephraim	5
Addams, Jane	15, 41, 62, 63
African Peace Research Institute. APRI Newsletter	89
Agency, The. World Military Expenditures and ArmsTransfers	89
Ahlborn, Emil	16
All-America Anti-Imperialist League	76
All-India Preparatory Peace Committee	76
Allen, Theophilus	16
Allied and Associated Powers	3, 16
Allied Supreme Economic Council	61
Almanach de la Paix par le Droit	89
Almond, Nina	16
America First Committee	15, 17, 62, 72, 76
America First Committee. Fight for Freedom Committee	17
American Academic Association for Peace in the Middle East.	
Background Paper	89
Bulletin	89
Mideast Media Review	89
American Arbitration Association	76
American Association for Adult Education	76
American Association for International Reconciliation InternationalConciliation	89
American Bar Association. Committee on War Work	76
American Civil Liberties Union	17
American Committee for Struggle Against War	76
American Committee for the Outlawry of War	76
American Committee on War Finance	76
American Congress for Peace and Democracy	76
American Foundation	76
American Friends Fellowship Council	76
American Friends Reconstruction Unit	76
American Friends Service Committee	8, 15, 17, 59, 72, 76
Peace Service Bulletin	89
Regional Bulletin	89
American Friends Service Committee. Peace Education Committee.	
United States Anti-Apartheid Newsletter	90
American Friends Service Committee. Peace Information Service.	
Peace News Wire	90
American Jewish Committee	76
American League Against War And Fascism	18, 76
American League Action Bulletin	90
American League to Limit Armaments	76
American Legion	76
American Neutral Conference Committee	76
American Peace and Arbitration League	76
Bulletin	90

American Peace Award	76
American Peace Congress	77
American Peace Crusade	77
American Peace Crusader	90
American Peace Mobilization	77
APM Newscaster	90
APM Volunteer	90
Bulletin	90
Facts for Peace	90
Mobilize for Peace	90
News	90
American Peace Society	19, 77
Advocate of Peace	90
Annual Report	90
World Affairs	90
American Peace Society of Japan. Bulletin	90
American Peace Terms Committee	77
American Purpose	90
American Red Cross in Belgium	15
American Relief Administration	20, 60
American School Citizenship League	77
American School Peace League	77
American Society for Judicial Settlement of International Disputes	77
Judicial Settlement of International Disputes	90
American Songs of Peace	19
American Union Against Militarism	19, 77
Bulletin	91
American University Union in Europe. Peace Series	91
American Women's Peace Party	15
Americans for Peace	77
America's Town Meeting of the Air	19
Anglican Pacifist Fellowship	77
Annuaire des Associations Internationales pour la Paix et la Société des Nations	91
Annuaire du Mouvement Pacifiste	91
Anti-Conscription Committee	77
Anti-"Preparedness" Committee (See American Union Against Militarism)	
Anti-Enlistment League	77
Arbeitsstelle Friedensforschung. AFB Info	91
Arms Control and Disarmament	91
Arms Control and Disarmament Agency. U.S. Documents on Disarmament	77, 91
Arms of Friendship, Inc.	77
Arunachal Mission	77
World Peace	91
Association de la Paix Par le Droit.	
Le Paix par le Droit	91
Association for Peace Education	77
Association to Abolish War	7, 77
Balch, Emily Greene	20, 41
Baldwin, Roger	17
Baker, Elizabeth N.	19
Baker, George Barr	20
Bedford, Hastings William Sackville Russell, 12th Duke	20
Bell, Johannes	21

Better World Club 77
Better World Fund 77
Bias, News-Peace, Integrity, Cooperation 91
Bibliotheque Pacifiste Internationale 77
Biosophical Review 91
Bliss, Tasker H. 21
Books for Peace and Freedom 91
Botha, Louis 21, 55
Boushall, Thomas C. 21
Brandt, Willy 37
Brandt, Zoia G. 62
Brest-Litovsk, Treaty of 34
Brethren Service Commission. (Brethren Service Committee) 77
Briggs, Mitchell Pirie 21
Broughton, Nicholas 22
Buffalo Peace and Arbitration Society 7, 77
    Executive Committee. Report 91
Bureau International Permanent de la Paix 77
Bureau of International Peace 41
Bureau of the World Peace Mission 77
Butler, Charles A. 22
California State Conference Against War and Fascism 77
Campaign For Nuclear Disarmament 22, 77
    Sanity. Voice of C.N.D. 91
Campaign for Peace and Democracy.
    Peace and Democracy News 91
Canadian Disarmament Information Service 77
    Peace Calendar 92
    Peace Magazine 92
Canadian Institute for International Peace and Security 77
    Annual Report 92
    Background Paper 92
    Guide to Canadian Policies on Arms Control, Disarmament,Defense, and Conflict Resolution . 92
    Peace and Security 92
    Peace in our time? 92
Canadian Peace Congress. Peace News 92
Canadian Peace Research Institute 77
    Peace Research 92
    Peace Research Abstracts Journal 92
    Peace Research Reviews 92
Carnegie, Andrew 23
Carnegie Endowment for International Peace 22, 23, 71, 77
    Annual Report 93
    Brief Reference List 92
    Epitome of the Purpose, Plans 93
    Year Book 93
Carnegie Endowment for International Peace. Division of Economics and History.
    Annual Report of the Director 92
Carnegie Endowment for International Peace. Division of Intercourse and
Education. Annual Report of the Director 92
Carnegie Endowment for International Peace. Division of International Law.
    Monograph Series 92
Carnegie Endowment for International Peace. Library.

Memoranda Series	92
Catholic Association for International Peace	78
Catholic Association for International Peace. Committee on Ethics	78
C.A.I.P. News	93
Catholic Pacifists' Association	78
Catt, Carrie Chapman	23
Center for Peace Studies. International Peace StudiesNewsletter	93
Center for Research on World Political Institutions	78
Center for the Study of Armament and Disarmament	78
Center for the Study of Democratic Institutions	78
Bulletin	93
Center Magazine	93
Center Report	93
Report of the President	93
Center for War/Peace Studies	78
Global Report	93
Center, The. Positive Alternatives	93
Center, The (New York). Deadline	93
Central Board for Conscientious Objectors	78
Central Committee for Conscientious Objectors	78
Central Organization For a Durable Peace	78
Centre de Documentation et de Recherche Sur la Paix et les Conflicts. Damocles	93
Centre Interdisciplinaire de Recherches Sur la Paix et d'Etudes Strategiques. Paix et Conflits	93
Centro de Estudios de Movimientos Sociales. A Priori	93
Centro de Información del Consejo Mundial de La Paz Para America y el Caribe. Cuban Movement for Peace and Sovereignty of thePeoples	93
Challenge of Disarmament	93
Chicago Committee to Oppose Peacetime Conscription	78
Chicago Committee to Win the Peace	78
Chicago Council of American-Soviet Friendship	78
Chicago Peace Society	78
Chinese Civil War	63
Chinese Communist Party	66
Chinese Students Association	78
Democratic Youth	93
Christian Action Movement	78
Christian Brotherhood Movement	78
Christian Conference on War and Peace	78
Christian Front for Peace Against Fascism	78
Christian Pacifists in California	78
Christian Peace Conference	78
Christol, Carl Quimby	24
Church of Brethren	8, 24
Church of England Peace League	78
Annual Report	94
Church Peace Union (see also, Council on Religion and International Affairs)	78
Churchmen's Committee for a Christian Peace	78
Citizens for Victory	78
Citizens Keep America Out of War Committee	78,79
Citizens Peace Petition Committee	78

Civilian Public Service	18, 27
Civilian Public Service Camp	22
Civilian Public Service Records	18
Civilian Public Service Union	24, 25, 26, 27
Clark, Harold A.	27
Clearing House for Limitation of Armament	78
Cole, Betty	18, 27
Collegiate Anti-Militarism League	78
War?	94
Collins, Ernest	27
Columbia University	2
Columbia University Youth Committee Against War	79
Comité Espagnol pour la Paix Civile	79
La Paix Civile	94
Commission for Relief in Belgium (CRB)	3, 20
Commission on a Just and Durable Peace	79
Commission on Christian Education	79
Commission on Christian Social Action	79
Commission on International Justice and Goodwill	79
Commission on Polish Affairs. Peace Conference, Paris, 1919	
Rapport	94
Commission on the Coordination of Efforts for Peace	79
Commission on World Peace of the Methodist Church	79
Commission to Study the Bases of a Just and Durable	79
Commission to Study the Organization of Peace	79
Broadcasts	94
Report	94
Committee for a Democratic Far Eastern Policy	79
Committee for Legal Aid to Conscientious Objectors	79
Committee for National Morale	79
Committee for Nonviolent Action	79
Committee for Peace Day in the United Nations	79
Committee for Peaceful Alternatives	79
Committee on Drafting Youth	79
Committee on Education for International Goodwill. The Teachers' Union Auxiliary	79
Committee on Education for Lasting Peace. Backlog for Action	94
Committee on Militarism in Education	27
Committee on Militarism in the Schools	79
Committee on Public Information	79
Committee to Defend America	79
Committee to Defend America by Aiding the Allies	79
Committee to Defend America by Keeping Out of War	79
Committee to Oppose Conscription of Women	79
Committee to Study the Basis of a Just and Durable Peace	79
Communist Information Bureau	10
For a Lasting Peace, for a People's Democracy	94
Communist International	79
Communist Party. Great Britain. Peace Library	94
Communist Party. United States (CPUSA)	18, 71
Community Relations Service	79
Concours Europeen de la Paix	79
Conference for Democracy and Terms of Peace	79

122

Conference for the Limitation of Naval Armament 28
Conference for the Reduction and Limitation of Armaments.
　Records of the Conference for the Reduction and Limitation of Armaments. Series A.
　Verbatim Records of Plenary Meetings 94
Conference of Clergymen of All Christian Churches 79
Conference of Naval Armament 7
Conference on Cause and Cure of War 79
Conference on Christian Pacifists 79
Conference on the Limitations of Armaments 7
Conference on Pacifist Philosophy of Life 80
Conference on Peace Research in History and the Consortium on Peace Research,
　Education and Development 80
　Peace and Change 94
Conference on Science, Philosophy and Religion in their Relation to the
　Democratic Way of Life. Symposium 94
Conference on the Discontinuance of Nuclear Tests 28
　Verbatim Record of the 1st Plenary 94
Conference to Plan a Strategy for Peace 80
Conferencia Interamericana Sobre Problemas de la Guerra y de la Paz
　Diario 94
Congregational Education Society 80
Congrès Mondial Contre la Guerre Imperialiste 80
Conscientious objectors 8, 18, 22, 24, 27, 32, 68, 78-79, 82-84, 107
Consultation on Christian Concern for Peace 80
Coolidge, Calvin 20
Cornell University 2
Coste, Brutus 28
Council on Religion and International Affairs. (see also, Church Peace Union)
　Report 95
Crummey, John D. 4
Cultural and Scientific Conference for World Peace 80
Curran, Edward Lodge 28
Current Articles, Interviews and Statements on Disarmament, PeacefulCoexistence
　and International Cooperation 94
Current Military Literature 95
Current Thought on Peace and War 94
D'Annunzio, Gabriel 63
D.A.R. Committee of Protest 80
Danielopol, Dumitru 28
Darlington, Charles F. 29
De 3E Weg 95
De Weg Naar Vrede 95
Defense de la Paix 95
Dekay, John Wesley 29
Delaware Peace Society 80
Democratic Party 29
Democratic Party. National Committee 80
Deutsche Friedens-Gesellschaft 34, 80
Deutsche Gesellschaft für Friedens und Konfliktforschung.
　DGFK Informationen 95
　DGFK-Jahrbuch 95
Deutscher Friedenskongress 80
Deutscher Friedensrat.

Information from the Peace Movement of the German DemocraticRepublic 95
Deutsches Friedenskomitee 80
　Friedenswacht 95
Disarmament 95
Disarmament and Arms Control 95
Disarmament Education Committee 80
Disarmament Information Committee 80
Division of Peace and World Order. General Board of Christian Social
　Concerns of the Methodist Church 80
Dodd, Norris E. 29
Dokumentation zur Abrustung und Sicherheit 95
Dole, Charles Fletcher 30
Don Cossacks, Province of the 30
Drayton, William A. 30
Drenikoff, Kyril 30
Dresser, Robert B. 31
Duke University 2
Duluth Peace Committee 80
Dunford House Cobden Memorial Association 31, 80
Dyer, Susan Louise 31
East Germany 48
Eckhardt, William 31
Economic and Disarmament Information Committee 80
Ecumenical Council of churches in Czechoslovakia, Prague.
　Christian Peace Conference 95
Emergency Peace Campaign 80
Episcopal Pacific Fellowship 80
Equitist League 80
European Subject Collection 31, 32
Evans, Arthur Maybury 32
Fackert, Harold E. 32
Federal Council of the Churches of Christ in America 80
Federation of International Polity Clubs 80
Fellowship of Reconciliation 2, 8, 32, 80
　California Newsletter 96
　The Gist 95
　Monthly News Sheet 95
　News Sheet 95
　Northern California Reports. News Series 96
　Northern California Reports. Quote Series 96
　Northern California Reports. Research Series 96
　Peace Notes 95
　Peacemaker 96
　Reconciliation 96
Fellowship of Youth for Peace 80
　Bulletin 96
Field, Herbert Haviland 32
Fielitz, Axel Von 33
Fight for Peace and Democracy (also, Fight AgainstWar and Fascism) 96
Food for Peace Program 64
Foerster, Friedrich Wilhelm 42
Ford, Henry 41
Foreign Economic Administration, Technical Industrial Disarmament Committee.

T.I.D.C. Project	96
Foreign Policy Association	80
Foreign Policy Committee Reports	96
Forschungsinstitut für Friedenspolitik.	
Friedens Brief	96
Foundation for P.E.A.C.E. Peace in Action	96
Foundation for Promoting Enduring Peace	80
Frank, Coleman	33
Frank, Karl Boromaus	33
Fredsposten	96
Free Religious Association of America	80
Free, Arthur M.	33
French Deterrence	34
Fried, Alfred Hermann	6, 34
Der Friedens Kampfer	80
Die Friedens-Warte	96
Friedensblätter des Verbandes Deutscher Handlunggehilfen zuLeipzig	96
Der Friedensbote	96
Der Friedensfreund	96
Friedensglocke	96
Friedensrat der Deutschen Demokratischen Republik	80
Der Friedensruf	96
Friedenszeitung	96
Friends Ambulance Unit	80
Friends Committee on National Legislation	35, 80
Annual Report	97
FCNL Action	97
Washington Newsletter	97
Friends of Kenya. Friends of Kenya	97
Friends of Peace	80
Friends Service Committee	81
Friends, Society of	35, 72
Friends World Conference Committee	81
Friends' Peace Service Letter	97
Furlong, Charles Wellington	35
Gaceta de Paz	97
Galsworthy, John	63
Gay, Edwin Francis	35
Geneva Disarmament Conference	45, 65, 69
German Peace Society (Deutsche Friedensgesellschaft)	34, 58, 80
Germany. Auswaertiges Amt	36
Gibson, Hugh	36
Golden Rule Foundation	81
Graham, Malbone	36
Great Britain. War Office. Daily Review of the ForeignPress	97
Great Lakes International Arbitration Society	81
Greater Philadelphia Committee Against Peacetime Conscription	81
Grin, J.	37
Grose, Ada Morse	6, 37
Grossmann, Kurt Richard	37
Grubbs, Frank Leslie	37
Hague International Peace Conference	33, 81
Hague Peace Conference, 1899-1907	40

Hasl, Franz Joseph 38
Henry Ford Peace Expedition 6, 39, 47, 63, 81
Henry Ford Peace Ship Expedition 54
Henry Ford's Neutral Conference 81
Herald of Peace 97
Herald of Peace and International Arbitrations 97
Herman, Raphael 38
Herron, George D. 22, 38
Herter, Christian Archibald 38
Hessische Stiftung Friedens und Konfliktforschung.
  Friedensgutachten 97
Hitler, Adolf 60
Hollingsworth, Sidney Pierce 39
Hollywood Peace Forum 97
Hoover, Henry 39
Hoover, Herbert 2, 3, 4, 6, 17, 20, 21, 31, 38, 39, 41, 55, 63
Hoover, Lou Henry 31
Hoover Institution 1, 3, 4, 5, 8, 10, 44, 46, 50, 66, 70
The Idealist: for Democracy, Peace, Race Tolerance 97
Imperial War Museum 3
Independent Labour Party, London. Women's Peace Crusade 97
Independent Labour Party, Manchester. Road to Peace 97
Institut Francais de Polemologie
  Etudes Polemologiques 98
  Guerres et Paix 98
Institut für Friedensforschung WienerBlätter Zur Friedensforschung 98
Institut für Gesellschaftswissenschaften 81
Institute, The Points of View 98
Institute for Defense Analyses 81
  Annual Report 98
  Research Paper 98
Institute for Humane Studies 81
Institute for International Order 81
Institute for the Study of Nonviolence. Journal 98
Institute of International Peace Studies 81
Institutt for Fredsforskning, Norway. Journal of PeaceResearch 98
Interamerican Conference for the Maintenance of Peace 81
Intercollegiate Peace Association 81
Intergovernmental Conference for the Conclusion of an International
  Convention Concerning the Use of Broadcasting in the Cause of
  Peace 81
International Arbitration and Peace Association 81
International Arbitration League 81
International Committee for Immediate Mediation 39, 47
International Conference for Disarmament and Peace, London.
  Peace Press 98
International Conference of Women Workers to Promote
  Permanent Peace 81
International Conference on World Peace 81
International Congress of Women 39, 63
International Convocation on the Requirements of Peace 81
International Dialogue 98
International Freedom Foundation. Angola Peace Monitor 98

International Institute for Peace	81
Current Documents and Papers on International ProblemsRelative to World Peace	98
International Key Bureau	81
International Labour Office. Official Bulletin	98
International Labour Organisation	7
International Peace Academy Committee	58, 81
International Peace Bureau. Berne	98
Correspondence Bi-Mensuelle	98
Die Friedensbewegung	98
Peace Information Bulletin	98
The Peace Movement	99
Procés-Verbal des Seances de la Commission duBureau	99
Rapport de Gestion pour l'Année	99
International Peace Bureau. Geneva Geneva Peace Monitor	99
International Peace Campaign	81
Meddelande	99
News Letter	99
Peace	99
Verksamhetsberuttelse	99
International Peace Conference	40
International Peace Congress	81, 99
International Peace Forum	81
International Peace Research Association	81
International Peace Research Newsletter	99
Science et Paix	99
International Peace Research Institute	81
Bulletin of Peace Proposals	99
International School of Peace	82
International Studies Conference	40
International Union	82
International Women's League	20
Internationales Institut für den Frieden	82
Inter-parliamentary Union	82
Aarbog for de Nordiske InterparlamentariskeGrupper	100
Annuaire de l'Union Interparliamentaire	100
Meddelelser Fra de NordiskeInterparlamentariske Grupper	100
Israel at Peace	100
Jahrbuch für Volkerrecht und Friedensbewegung	100
Jansen, B. Douglass	40
Japan Peace Society	82
Jewish-Arab Association for Peace and Equality.	
Bulletin	100
Johnson, Douglas	40
Jordan, David Starr	6, 10, 29, 37, 40, 41
Journal of Conflict Resolution	100
Jünger, Ernst	41
June Calahan Foundation	82
Karmin, Otto	42
Kaslas, Bronis J.	42
Keep America Out of War Congress.	82
War, What For	100
Kerensky, Aleksandr	60, 63
Kertess, Stephen D.	42

Kissinger, Henry A. 34
Kittredge, Tracy Barrett 42
Kleinhaus, Eleanor M. 43
Klub der Deutschen Sozialdemokratischen Abgeordneten.
   Die Taetigkeit der Deutschen SozialdemokratischenAbgeordnetenim Oesterreichischen Reichsrat 100
Koestner, Nicolai 42
Konrad-Adenauer-Stiftung. Die Frau in Unserer Zeit 100
Kropotkin, Petr 41
Krupenskii, Aleksandr Nikolaevich 43
Lafayette Institute 82
Lansing, Robert 43
Latin American Subject Collection 44
Latin American Institute 82
League for an American Peace (See American Union Against Militarism)
League for Industrial Democracy. Disarm! 100
League for World Peace 82
League of Peace and Freedom 82
League for Permanent Peace 82
League for World Federation 82
League for World Peace. Journal 100
League of Nations 7, 16, 29, 36, 38, 39, 43, 44, 55, 56, 57,
   59, 60, 65, 67, 74
   Covenant . . . 22
   International Trade Statistics 100
   Journal Officiel 100
   Memorandum on International Trade and Balance ofPayments 100
   Memorandum on Public Finance 100
   Money and Banking 100
   Monthly Summary of the League of Nations 100
   Report on the Work of the League 100
   Statistical Yearbook of the Trade in Arms, Ammunitions,and Implements of War 101
   Work of the Health Organization 101
   Yearbook of the League of Nations 101
League of Nations Commission of Enquiry in Manchuria 54
League of Nations Union 82
League of Peace and Freedom 82
League of Women Voters 45
League to Enforce Peace 60, 82
   League Bulletin 101
Library of the Peace Palace. The Hague 82
Lindberg, Charles 17
Life and Peace Institute. Life and Peace Review 101
Liverpool Peace Society 82
Lloyd George, David 45
Lobby for Peace 82
Lockley, Fred 45
Logan, James Addison, Jr. 45
London Naval Conference 46, 65, 69
Loucheur, Louis 46
Lutz, Ralph Haswell 16
McCormick, Vance C. 46
Malik, Charles Habib 46, 47
Manuila, Sabin 46

Marx, Charles D. 16
Marx, Guido Hugo 47
Maryland Peace Society 82
   Maryland Quarterly 101
Masaryk, Tomas 42, 63
Masland, John Wesley, Jr. 47
Massachusetts Peace Society 82
Maverick, Lewis A. 47
Medical Association for Prevention of War.
   Journal 101
   Proceedings 101
Medical Peace Campaign. Bulletin 101
Mehring, Franz 47
Mennonite Peace Problems Committee 82
The Messenger for Peace 101
Methodist Church 82
Mid-Peninsula Peace Center Peaceworks 101
Miflaga Komunistit Yisraelit (MAKI).
   Information Bulletin 101
Miller, David Hunter 5, 48
Millis, Walter 48
Ministers' No War Committee 82
Mir 101
Mir Chez Suiuziavane 101
Mir Ctvrtletnik Pro Obranu Miru 101
Mir i Razoruzhenie 101
Mohsell, Irmela 48
Monetary and Economic Conference 48
Moran, Hugh Anderson 48
Morse, John H. 49
Mount Holyoke Institute on the United Nations.
   Selected Speeches 101
Movimiento Cubano por la Paz y la Soberania de los Pueblos
   Sintesis Informativa 102
Munro, Dana Carleton 49
Musee de la Geurre 3
National Catholic Welfare Conference 82
National Citizens' Commission on International Cooperation 82
National Civic Federation 82
National Civil Liberties Bureau 82
National Committee Against Peacetime Conscription Now 82
National Committee on Conscientious Objectors 68, 82
National Committee on the Cause and Cure of War 82
National Congress of Peace and Friendship With the U.S.S.R. 82
National Council Against Conscription 82
National Council for Civil Liberties 82
National Council for Conscientious Objectors 83
National Council for Reduction of Armaments 83
National Council for the Prevention of War 49, 83
   International Notes for Disarmament and WorldRecovery 102
   News Bulletin 102
   Peace Action 102
   Peace Voter News 102

Peacemaker	102
Report	102
Report Letter	102
Report on Naval Conference	102
Washington Information Letter	102
National Council of Returned Peace Corps Volunteers.	
Worldview Magazine	102
National Council to Abolish War	83
National Education Association of the United States	83
National Emergency Committee	83
National Federation of Temple Sisterhoods	83
Peace News Flashes	102
National Inter-Religious Conference on Peace	83
National Legation of the American People	83
National Peace Conference	83
Annual Report	102
Bulletin	102
Geneva Information	102
Inter-council News Letter	102
Washington Information Service	103
World Affairs Pamphlets	103
National Peace Conference. Committee on Economics and Peace	83
National Peace Conversion Campaign	83
National Peace Council	50, 83
Economic Series	102
Educational Series	103
General Series	103
International Declarations	103
Monthly Circular	103
NPC Papers	103
One World	103
Peace	103
Peace Aims Documents	103
Peace Aims Pamphlets	103
Peace Year Book	103
Political Series	103
Report	103
Social Reform Series	103
Towards World Government	103
National Peace Council. Information Office.	
American Opinion	103
Reading and Reference Notes	104
National Peace Council of New Zealand.	
Monthly Circular	104
National Peace Federation	83
National Peace Literature Service	83
National Republic Magazine	50
National Security League	10, 50, 83
Bulletin	104
General Letter	104
Patriotism Through Education Series	104
Report	104
Research Bulletin	104

National Service Board for Religious Objectives 83
National Spiritual Assembly of the Baha'is of the U.S. and Canada 83
National Student Committee for the Limitation of Armament 83
National Student Forum on the Paris Pact 83
Neutral Conference for Continuous Mediation 6, 37, 39, 47
   Neutral Conference Documents 103
New England Arbitration and Peace Congress 83
New England Citizens Concerned for Peace 83
New Hampshire Peace Society 83
New History Foundation 83
New History Society 83
New Left Collection 8, 50
New York Peace Association 83
New York Peace Information Center. Where in the World? 104
New York Peace Information Service.
   The Poor Man's Guide to War Man's Guide to War/PeaceLiterature 104
New York Peace Society 51, 83
   Messenger of the New York Peace Society 104
   News Letter 104
   Yearbook 104
New York Public Library 2
New York State War Council 83
   War Digest 104
New York Student Federation Against War 83
Newcombe, Alan G. 51
Newcombe, Hanna 51
Nicholas II, Tsar 66
Nixon, Richard M. 64
No Conscription Council 83
No More War Movement 83
Nobel, Alfred 7, 60
Nobel Peace Prize 6, 15, 18, 20, 34, 60
Non-Violent Action Against Nuclear Weapons 84
Non-Violent Action Committee 84
North Atlantic Treaty Organization 48, 49
Northern California Committee to Oppose Peacetime Conscription Now 84
Northern California Peace Society 84
Northern California Service Board for Conscientious Objectors 84
Novosti Press Agency. Disarmament and Security 104
Nowak, Bohdan 52
Nuclear Disarmament 104
Nuclear Times 104
Obiezione 104
Obshchestvo Mira y Moskie 104
Oesterreichische Friedensgesellschaft.
   Der Friedensfreund 104
Ohio Peace Committee 84
Oklahoma Committee Against Compulsory Military Training 84
Olivereau, Louise 52
Oppenheimer, Franz 41
L'Organisation Politique et Economique du Monde. La Paix desPeuples 104
Organization of American Women for Strict Neutrality 84
Oscar Arias Peace Plan 9

Ossietsky, Carl Von	37
Osusky, Stepan	52
Pace e Libertà	105
Pacific Studies Center	84
Pacifica Associates	84
Pacifica Center Associates of Los Angeles.	
Peace Digest	105
Pacifist Research Bureau	52
Quarterly Research Survey	105
Pacifistisch Socialistische Partij. Bevrijding	105
La Paix; Journal Libre Renseignant ...	105
La Paix. Journal Politique, d'Economie ...	105
La Paix Mondiale	105
La Paix Organisée	105
La Paix: Revue Internationale de Critique Pacifiste	105
Palo Alto Peace Club	84
Flashlight	105
Paris Conference To Consider the Draft treaties of Peace with Italy, Rumania, Bulgaria, Hungary, and Finland	52
Paris Peace Conference, 1919	5, 16, 20, 21, 30, 35, 36, 38, 40, 42, 43, 45, 46, 49, 53, 55, 61, 64, 66, 70
La Paix de Versailles	105
Preliminary Peace Conference	105
Recueil des Actes de la Conference	105
Commission on Baltic Affairs. Minutes	53
U.S. Division of Territorial, Economic and Political Intelligence	54
Paris Peace Conference, 1946	29, 42, 84
Park, Alice	6, 54, 56
Pastuhov, Vladimir D.	54
Patriotic Peace League	84
Peace Action Center	84
Peace Action Coalition	105
Peace Action Committee of Missouri	84
Peace Action Service	84
Peace and Arbitration Society of Buffalo, N.Y.	41
Peace and Disarmament Committee of the Women's International Organisations	84
Peace and Freedom News	105
Peace and Goodwill	105
Peace and Service Committee. Indiana Yearly Meeting of Friends	84
Peace Association of Friends in America. The Messenger ofPeace	105
Peace Ballot Commission	84
Peace Balloon	105
Peace Builders	84
Peace Campaign	84
Peace Committee of Philadelphia	84
Peace Committee of the National Council of Women	84
Peace Conference of the Asian and Pacific Regions	84
Peace Congress Committee	84
Peace Digest Associates	84
Peace Digest	106
Peace Heroes Memorial Society	85

Peace House	85
Peace Information Center	85
Peacegram	106
Peace News, New York	106
Peace News, St. Petersburg	106
Peace News for Nonviolent Revolution	106
Peace News, Ltd., London.	
Peace News: the International Pacifist Weekly	106
Peace Newsletter	106
Peace Now	106
Peace Now Movement	85
Peace Patriots	85
Arbitrator	106
Peace Pilgrims	85
Peace Plans (Berrima, Australia)	106
Peace Plans (Libertarian Microfiche Publications)	106
Peace Pledge Union	85
Bond of Peace	106
Peace News	106
Peace Posters	54
Peace Preparedness League	85
Preparedness	106
Peace Progress	106
Peace Research Institute	85
Journal of Peace Research	106
Peace Research Abstracts	106
Prif Reports	106
Peace Research Society International	85
Peace Societies of the District of Columbia.	
The Crisis	106
Peace Society of the City of New York	85
Peace Society. London.	85
Pamphlets on War and Peace	106
Peace Strategy Board	85
Peace Studies Institute	85
Bulletin	106
Peace Subject Collection	55
Peace Union of Finland	85
Peacemaker Movement. Peacemaker	106
Peacemakers	85
Pennington, Levi Talbott	55
Pennsylvania Arbitration and Peace Society	85
Pennsylvania Committee for Total Disarmament	85
Pennsylvania Peace Society	85
People for Peace	85
People's Congress for Democracy and Peace	85
Congress Builder	106
People's Council of America	56, 85
Bulletin	106
People's Council of America for Democracy and Peace	85
People's Freedom Union	85
People's Mandate Committee for Inter-American Peace and Cooperation	85

People's Mandate Committee to End War 85
People's Peace 85
Permanent International Armistice Commission 33
Petrescu-Comnen, Nicolae 56
Philadelphia Youth Council to Oppose Conscription 85
Physical Education Committee of Pennsylvania 85
Piip, Antonius 56
Plea for Peace 85
Pledge for Peace Committee 85
Pokoj i Wolnosc. Paix et Liberté 107
Poland. Ambasada 56
Poland. Ministerstwo Prac Kongresowych 57
Poland. Ministerstwo Prac Kongresowych. Rada Morska 57
Poland. "Solidarity Collection." 57
Popovskii, Mark Aleksandrovich 58
Portland Women's Peace Council 85
Post War Bureau, London. War and Peace Aims Digest 107
Post War World Council 85
Pravda 58
Problemas de la Paz y del Socialismo 107
Prison Views 107
Professors World Peace Academy. PWPA International SpecialReport 107
Promoting Enduring Peace 85
Pusta, Kaarel Robert 58
Quidde, Ludwig 58
Radisics, Elemer 59
Rationalist Peace Society 85
Reclus, Elisée 42
Reed, Howard A. 59
Religious Society of Friends 86
Republican Party 20
Requin, Edouard Jean 59
Research Institute for Peace and Security.
   Asian Security 107
Respect for Life. World Peace Press 107
Revue des Balkans: Politique. Diplomatique. Finances 107
Rhodes, Cecil 63
Richardson, Grace 59
Rieffel, Aristide 60
Riga, Treaty of 60
Rijksuniversiteit te Groningen Polemologisch Instituut. Assen, Netherlands.
   Nieuwe Literatuur Over Oorlog en Vrede 107
Ringland, Arthur C. 60
Ritter, Gerhard 60
Robinson, Henry Mauris 61
Roosevelt, Theodore 41
Root, Elihu 50
Rotary International 86
Rothwell, Charles Easton 61
Ruestung und Abruestung 107
Russia. Posol'stvo (France) 61
Sacramento Peace Center. Peace Currents 107
San Jose Peace Center. Peace Times 107

Sanity. Peace-Oriented News and Comment 107
Sapon'ko, Angel Osipovich 62
Sarles, Ruth 62
Schmidt, Frieda 62
Schuder, Kurt 62
Schweizerische Friedensbewegung 86
Schwimmer, Rosika 6, 41, 62
Scientific Research Council on Peace and Disarmament 86
Shanghai Peace Delegation 63
Shaw, John Putnam 63
Shishmanian, John Amar 63
Sicherheit und Friedliche Zusammenarbeit in Europa 107
Sinclair, Upton 41
Sipri Yearbook of World Armaments and Disarmament 108
Slosson, Preston W. 64
Socialist Party 86
    Committee on Education and Research 86
    Committee for the Third International 86
Società Internationale Per la Pace. Pro Pace 108
Société de la Paix de Moscou. Obshchestvo Mira vMoskvie 108
Société pour l'Arbitrage Entre Nations. Revue de laPaix 108
Society for Social Responsibility in Science. S.S.R.S.Newsletter 108
Society for the Prevention of WWIII 86
Society for the Promotion of Permanent and Universal Peace 86
Society of Friends, Great Britain 86
South Dakota Peace Society 86
Soviet Peace Committee 86
    The Twentieth Century and Peace 108
Spitzer, Robert R. 64
Stanford, Barbara Dodds 64
Stanford Draft Counseling Office 64
Stanford University 8, 40, 70, 71, 72, 73
    Alumni Association of Tokyo 8
Stanley Foundation.
    Conference to Plan a Strategy for Peace. Report 108
    US Foreign Policy Conference. Strategy for Peace 108
Statements on War and Peace Aims 107
Stockholm International Peace Research Institute 86
    The Arms Race and Arms Control 108
Stowell, Ellery Cory 64
Strategy for Peace 86
Street, Cyrus H. 55, 65
Strong, Sydney 45, 65
Student Fellowship for Christian Life Service 86
Student Mobilisation Committee to End the War in Vietnam 86
Student Peace Service 86
    Peace Points 108
Student Peace Union 86
Students for a Democratic Society 65
Sudan. Southern Region. Ministry of Information, Culture, Youth, and Sports.
    Peace and Progress 108
Sumans, Vilis 65
Suttner, Bertha von 6, 7, 34, 37, 65

Swarthmore College Peace Collection 2, 72, 73
   Peace Collection Bulletin 107
Swingle, John 19
Sworakowski, Witold S. 66
Ta Chung Cultural Cooperation Association 66
Taft, William Howard 41
Tampere Peace Research Institute.
   Current Research on Peace and Violence 108
   Instant Research on Peace and Violence 108
Tapri Yearbook 108
Thoennings, Johan 66
Tittle, Walter 66
Titulescu, Nicolae 66
Tolstoyan Pacifist Movement 58
Tract Association of Friends 86
True, Arnold 67
Truth About Preparedness Committee (See American Union Against Militarism)
Ulster Association for Peace with Honour. The UlsterBulletin 108
Unidad de Información. Programa de Apoyo a la Paz, la Cooperación y el
   Desarrollo en Centroamerica. Documentos 108
Union for Democratic Control 86
Unitarian Pacifist Fellowship 86
United Brotherhood Tolerance Movement 86
United Italy Society of Great Britain. Problems of the PeaceCongress 109
United Mothers World Peace Movement 86
United Nations 8, 12, 29, 44, 46, 47, 74
   Centre Against Apartheid. International Mobilization 109
   Centre for Disarmament. Disarmament Yearbook 109
   Conference of the Committee on Disarmament.
      Basic Information for Delegations on Conference Arrangements and Documents 109
      Checklist of Documents 109
      Final Verbatim Record 109
      List of Members of Delegations to the Conference 109
   Conference on International Organization 67
   Dept. for Disarmament Affairs. Disarmament Newsletter 109
   Educational, Scientific, and Cultural Organiation 71
      UNESCO Yearbook On Peace and ConflictStudies 109
   General Assembly. Committee on Disarmament at U.N. Headquarters.
      Disarmament Times 109
   Preparatory Commission of the United Nations 68
United Nations General Assembly and Disarmament 109
United Pacifist Committee 86
United Peace Chest 86
U.S. Arms Control and Disarmament Agency 40, 86
   Arms Control Report 109
   Documents on Disarmament 109
   Publication 110
   World Military Expenditures and Arms Trade 110
   World Military Expenditures and Related Data 110
U.S. Army. Board of Inquiry 68
U.S. Congress. Senate. Committee on Foreign Relations.
   Neutrality, Peace Legislation, and Our ForeignPolicy 110
U.S. Council of National Defense 61

U.S. Department of State 68, 74
   Disarmament Document Series 110
   Disarmament Series 110
United States Institute of Peace. United States Institute of PeaceJournal 110
U.S. Office of Disarmament and Arms Control 63
U.S. Selective Service System. 68
United World Federalists 86
   The Student Federalist 110
Universal Peace Union 86
   The Peacemaker and Court of Arbitration 110
Universitets for Laget, Oslo, Norway. Bulletin of Peace 110
Universities Committee on Post-War International Problems.
   Problems 110
University of California. Associated Students. Peace Committee 86
University of New Brunswick. Center for Conflict Studies 87
   Conflict Quarterly 110
University of Sussex. Armament and Disarmament Information Unit.
   ADIU Report 110
Utsunomiya Gunshuku Kenkyushitsu. Gunshuku Fmondai Shiry O 110
V Zashchiut Mira 110
Vaihinger, Hans 42
Van Keuren, Alexander Hamilton 69
Vanderhoof, Frank E. 68
Verlag Wissenschaft und Politik. Koelner Ringvorlesung su Fragen von Frieden und Krieg . . 110
Via Pacis 110
Vietnam War 8, 43, 51, 65, 74
Voice of Peace 69
Vsemirnyi Kongress Storonnikov Mira. Postoiannyi Komitet.
   Mir 111
Vsesoiuznaia Konferentsiia Storonnikov Mira 87
War/Peace Report 111
War Resisters' International 69
War Resisters' League 2, 69, 87
   The Nonviolent Activist 111
   W.R.L. News 111
   Win 111
Warden, A.A. 69
Washington D.C. Conference on the Limitation of Armament 55, 66
Webster, Daniel 19
Wegerer, Alfred Von 70
White, Andrew 2
White, Henry 70
Wilhelm II, Kaiser 63
Williams, Mary Wilhelmine 70
Willis, Bailey 71
Wilson, Howard E. 71
Wilson, Woodrow 22, 35, 38, 41, 46, 60, 63
Wisbech Local Peace Association. Reports 111
Wisconsin Historical Society 2
Wisconsin Peace Society 87
Wissmann, Hellmuth, B. 71
Witness for Peace. What We Have Seen and Heard inNicaragua 111
Wolfe, Bertram David 71

Woman's Christian Temperance Union 87
Woman's Peace Party 72, 87
Woman's Republic 87
Women's Committee for World Disarmament 87
Women's Committee to Oppose Conscription 87
Women's International Democratic Federation.
   Information Bulletin 111
   Unity for the Defence of Our Rights, of Our Children, ofPeace 111
Women's International League for Peace and Freedom 2, 10, 15, 20,
   41 70, 72, 73
   British Section. Monthly News Sheet 111
   British Section. Yearly Reports 111
   Danish Section. Fred Od Frihed 111
   Geneva. Bulletin 111
   Geneva. Circular Letters 111
   Geneva. International Congress of the Women's InternationalLeague for Peace and Freedom . 111
   Geneva. International News 112
   Geneva. News Letter from Geneva 112
   Geneva. Pax Special 112
   German Section. Völkerversöhnende.
   Frauenarbeit 112
   9th Congress. Circular Letter on Congress 112
   Norwegian Section. Fred og Frihet 112
   Swedish Section. Arsber Attelse 112
   Swedish Section. Fredoch och Frihet 112
   United States Section. Annual Report 112
   United States Section. Boston. News of the United StatesSection 111
   United States Section. Bulletin 112
   United States Section. CA State Branch. Bulletin 112
   United States Section. Chicago. Yearbook 111
   United States Section. Labor Letter 112
   United States Section. Los Angeles Branch. PeaceBrevities 113
   United States Section. New York. News Sheet 113
   United States Section. New York. International CircularLetter 113
   United States Section. Peace and Freedom 112
   United States Section. Washington, D.C. Four Lights 113
   United States Section. Washington, D.C. Washington Newsletter 113
Women's International Organisation. Peace and Disarmament Committee.
   Annual Report 113
   Press Release 113
Women's National Committee to Keep U.S. out of War 87
Women's Peace Society 87
   News Letter 113
Women's Peace Union 87
Women's Trade Union League of America 20
   The Word in the Service of an Understanding Between AllMankind 113
The Word in the Service of an Understanding Between all.
   Mankind 113
World Anti-Communist League 30
World Alliance for International Friendship Through the Churches 87
World Assembly for Peace 87
World Citizens Assembly. World Citizen 113
World Citizens Association 87

World Committee Against War and Fascism 87
World Committee of Partisans of Peace 87
World Conference for International Peace Through Religion 87
  Publication 113
World Conference of Representatives of National Peace Movements 87
World Conference on World Peace through the Rule of Law.
  World Peace Through Law 113
World Congress Against War 87
World Council of Peace 87
  Bulletin 113
  Documents 113
  Information Bulletin 113
  Perspectives 113
World Court 7
World Federalist Association. World Federalist 113
World Festival of Youth and Students for Peace and Friendship.
  Information Bulletin 113
World Liberalism 87
World Order 113
World Pacifist Meeting 87
World Peace Assembly 87
World Peace Association 87
  World Government Advocate 113
World Peace Congress at Glasgow 58
World Peace Congress, Paris. Les Partisans de la Paix 114
World Peace Congress, Paris. Los Partidarios de la Paz 114
World Peace Congress, Paris. World Peace Congress Bulletin 114
World Peace Congress, Prague Section. World Peace CongressBulletin 114
World Peace Council 74
  Peace Courier 114
  Information Centre. Programme of Action 114
World Peace Foundation 87
  America Looks Ahead 114
  Annual Report 114
  Documents on American Foreign Relations 114
  Studies in Citizen Participation in InternationalRelations 114
  World Affairs Books 114
World Peace Library Association. The Mace Bulletin 114
World Peace Newsletter 114
World Peace Prize 63
World Peace Report 114
World Peace Stamp 87
World Peaceways 87
  Bulletin 114
  Information Service 114
  The Neutral World 114
  Peaceways Forum 114
  World Observer 114
World Unity 114
World Veterans Federation. International Information Center on
  Peacekeeping Operations. Documentation 115
World Veterans Foundation. Disarmament 115
World War I 5, 16, 33, 36, 40, 43, 45, 46, 48-49, 52, 57, 59, 62-63,

71, 73
World War II 8, 15, 17, 36, 41, 44, 50, 56, 59, 62, 66, 70, 71
World Without War Council 74, 87
World Without War Council of Northern California 2, 74
World Youth Peace 87
Y.M.C.A.'s. Committee on Public Affairs of the National Council 87
Youth Committee Against War 88
   Anti-War News Service 115
Youth Movement for World Recovery 88
Za Mir i Besopasnost Naradov 115
Za Mir i Trud 115
Zilberman, Bella N. 75
Zionism, Enemy of Peace and Social Progress 115
Zorn, Phillip 75